A HAIRST O' WORDS

New Writing from North-East Scotland

Other Titles by AUP

A PLEASURE OF GARDENS
edited by Joyce and Maurice Lindsay

THE LAND OUT THERE
A Scottish Land Anthology
edited by George Bruce
with the assistance of Frank Rennie

GLIMMER OF COLD BRINE
A Scottish Sea Anthology
edited by Alistair Lawrie, Hellen Matthews, Douglas Ritchie

THE SCOTTISH DOG
edited by Joyce and Maurice Lindsay

THE SCOTTISH CAT
edited by Hamish Whyte

GRAMPIAN HAIRST
An Anthology of North-East Prose
edited by William Donaldson and Douglas Young

A HAIRST O' WORDS

New Writing from North-East Scotland

edited by
Hellen Matthews

foreword by
Iain Crichton Smith

ABERDEEN UNIVERSITY PRESS
Member of Maxwell Macmillan Publishing Corporation

First published 1991
Aberdeen University Press

British Library Cataloguing in Publication Data

A hairst o' words: new writing from the
North East of Scotland
I. Matthews, Hellen
820.800914

ISBN 0 08 041198 3

Typeset from author generated discs by
Hewer Text Composition Services
Printed by Athenaeum Press Ltd

Foreword

Two years ago I was one of the judges, along with Ken Morrice and Jessie Kesson, of an amateur writing competition sponsored by Bissets, the old-established Aberdeen bookseller. I am glad to see some of the stories I selected represented here, along with poems and reminiscences. All the pieces stand up very well to publication.

The reminiscence and memories make up most of the book, but one cannot call them simply nostalgic or sentimental, for their detail is so exact.

We read about schools, markets, the fishing, the land, the church, fine days and storms; father read from Charles Dickens; family worship is described; there were paraffin lamps; 'we stuck to the recently varnished pews'; janitors wore pill box hats. There is talk of 'my first grapefruit', 'my first telephone'. There were the rich and there were the poor. Young girls went into service and trembled on their first day at the big house. Herring girls or fisher lassies wore bandages on their hands because of the sharp salt biting into them. (My own mother was one of these.) 'Wet-legged and freezing fisherwomen carried their men on their backs from the boats.' The greyness of the sky was 'like dull light off a dogfish's back.' There were peat fires, and witches are imagined burning in the fires.

Some of the pieces are in Doric, some in English. (Most of them are in English). We are introduced to such words as 'stannies'. 'speldins', 'murlin', 'gansie' and 'burrock'. The latter two words appear in Gaelic under different spellings. Many Gaelic speakers were involved, of course, in fishing in the North-East.

The book is divided into sections – 'When We Were Young', 'The Land', 'The Sea', 'Folk' and 'A Sense of Place'. In the section 'Folk', we are brought up to date with a story about an encounter between a yuppie and a prostitute in Aberdeen.

This is a very fine anthology indeed, well and carefully chosen, unpretentious and detailed. It will bring back memories and not only to people of the North-East. It has the freshness which the best kind of amateur writing has. Blackberry juice stains the pinafore indelibly, one of the contributors writes, and this is a natural and social observation all in one.

I would think there would be rich dippings here for the sociologist, but nevertheless what distinguishes the collection is the personal quality of the writing, its rich linguistic resources, and its immediacy of lived detail.

Aberdeen University Press is doing good work with these anthologies. *Glimmer of Cold Brine* was an excellent one, and a new anthology of Scottish prose and poetry, *The Land Out There*, edited by George Bruce has been widely praised.

Iain Crichton Smith.

Contents

The illustrations on pp 2, 24, 50 and 80 are courtesy of Aberdeen Central Library, and the illustration on p 108 is courtesy of Donal McLaughlin.

COVER ILLUSTRATION:

Harvesting, Forest of Birse by Joseph Farquharson
Courtesy of City of Aberdeen Art Gallery and Museums Collection

Acknowledgements

In addition to all those whose entries for Bissets Writing competition provided me with the raw material of this Anthology, there are many other individuals to whom I owe my thanks. For help in my quest for illustrations I must thank the staff of Aberdeen City Libraries; Andrew Hills and his staff at Aden House Museum of Farming Life, Mintlaw; Dorothy Kidd, Librarian at the Scottish Ethnological Archive, Edinburgh; and Donal McLaughlin, Department of German, University of Aberdeen. I am also indebted to The Grampian Initiative for their generous contribution to the publishing costs of the Anthology, and to Iain Crichton Smith who, having already given his time as a judge of Bissets Writing Competition, most generously agreed to read the manuscript of the Anthology and write a Foreword. Thanks are also due to the board of Blackwells Bookshops for agreeing to sponsor the Writing Competition, to Tony Schmitz, Managing Director, Bissets, for having the good idea in the first place, and to Colin McLean, retired Managing Director, Aberdeen University Press, for encouraging him to pursue it. That this volume should ever have reached publication is a mark of the importance attached to active involvement in the arts in North-East Scotland. Finally, I am particularly indebted to Tony Schmitz for inviting me to become involved in what has been a most enjoyable project.

Hellen Matthews
July 1991
Aberdeen

WHEN WE WERE YOUNG

Pictures in the Fire

Pit oot the licht, I'll sit alane,
The peat fire glow is a' I need
Pictures noo without a frame,
They're a' here mirrored in my heid.

A country school—bairns walkin' miles
(Thae days we hadna even bikes!)
A gird tae rin ahin, an' whiles
A sledge fin winter filled the dykes.

Lang simmer days wi' barfit feet
Parks o' stooks an' wee hairst mice
A wild floo'er carpet, made complete,
Oor ain wee world ca'ed paradise.

A clockin' hen wi' a' her brood
Gings cluckin' roon an' scrapin' sair,
A feathered 'mum' but jist as prood,
Her day's her ain—she's free as air.

Ah weel—a bairn's life noo-adays
tae mine bears nae resemblance
But amang the gifts the guid Lord gies
There's ane he ca'ed remembrance.

S WINCHESTER

Portsoy

We had taken nearly three hours to reach Portsoy, and now the holidays
had really started. Long sunny days seemed to be our lot then, although I
have no doubt we had rain, but no real memories of that, except for the
fact that for such occasions the aunts had a wonderful cupboard in their

parlour which afforded us all sort of delights—books, jigsaw puzzles, board games, a lovely old musical box which played six tunes, a set of baskets which got smaller and smaller as we lifted each lid, sent home by an uncle as he travelled the world in his Clipper ship.

There were picnics, with tea carried in flasks, mugs packed in, everything carried along to the West Braes, the East Braes, Sandend, Saney-ee. We collected softies from the Baker which were buttered and jammed and tasted like nectar, so soft and fresh they were. I think the West Braes was our favourite spot: there we paddled and found jellyfish to play fishmongers' shops with, and lovely flat stones which could be anything we wanted them to be. We used to walk over to the West Braes right after breakfast, going through the town, and usually stopping at McIntyre's, the grocer, to get apples or perhaps a yellow melon, and if we were lucky old Mr McIntyre used to give us the dregs from jars which had contained boiled sweeties. Having partaken of these delights during the morning, we were exhorted not to tell our aunts that we had done so, or, at least, to eat all our dinner, otherwise we'd never get such a treat again!

As we found our way home for dinner, more than likely the clock in the church tower in Seafield Street would be striking 12 noon, and we quickened our pace so that we would be on time. The elder of my aunts was a grand cook! She made crumpets for tea and we often found special small ones made for us. My grandfather used to have a barrel of cider sent up from the Midlands and we children were allowed to turn the tap on the barrel and fill the jug, and woe betide us if we started complaining that one of us got more than the other when the golden fluid was poured into our glasses. There was always a special smell in the kitchen as my aunt used to cook on a paraffin stove. The house was lit then by paraffin lamps; lovely to us, they were not so popular with the aunt who had to clean them. We were sent up to bed by the light of candlesticks, and on our way there we passed the old Grandfather clock in the hall—and it is quite true that one of the aunts used to stop the clock at night, to save the tick!

MARGARET E SMITH

Wheeling and Dealing

My twin brother eventually became a banker but it was as children in Portsoy that he and I first carried out a business transaction, rather well, we thought!

An aunt who kept hens sent us off into the town with a basket of eggs which were to be sold to one of the grocers, but we very stupidly used our bikes and a few of the eggs got cracked. We pondered what on earth to do to put matters right, and hit on the idea of going down to the little burn nearby, throwing away the cracked eggs, washing the piece of flannel on which they had been resting, and then going to the other grocer in the town, where we bought four eggs with our own pocket money, added them to the original lot, and sold them to the first grocer as we had been meant to do. But, of course, the damp piece of flannel gave us away on our return and we had to own up!

MARGARET E SMITH

Church going

The kirk was over two miles by road from our home but only about a mile on foot through the fields and woods. From our row of houses came seven children of varying ages who set out each Sunday bedecked in their Sunday best ready to enjoy the walk to the kirk. We always left in good time as we had many things to do on the way: the black pony at the first farm had to have his piece; the blaeberries in the wood were worth stopping for; and the gooseberry bush at the old ruin just through the wood needed careful monitoring. To taste those gooseberries before they were ripe was an everlasting temptation, but we all knew to our cost that they had to be resisted until they were red and soft and could be savoured equally by all—a few on the way to Sunday school and a feast on the way home.

Another of our dallying grounds was the rookery. On our way to the kirk we gathered cones and left them in hidey holes ready to collect on the way home. Cones were carried home in some strange containers—jackets, hats, hankies were used and even stocking were taken off to use if nothing else was handy. We had countless hours of fun in that wood disturbing the rooks high in the trees. We shouted, yelled and whistled like banshees and threw cones at them just to see them circle round in a temper, their raucous protests warning the other children (who were converging on the kirk from all directions), that we were on our way. We always knew it was time to run when one bird, bolder than the others, started to dive-bomb us.

We usually arrived at the kirk sticky, dirty, out of breath and more than ready for the refreshment provided. This was a pail of cold water placed at the door of the kirk which we drank by using a ladle left hanging on the wall. That water tasted like sheer nectar.

One of our favourite walks was down a road where a so-called lady of ill-repute stayed—a woman well known for spreading her favours wide and well, and we frequently chanced upon the hopefully hidden bicycle of one of our church-going worthies there. We did everything we could think of to that bike. We hung it up in the trees, we immersed it in the burn, we let down the tyres and we tied it up with string. I sometimes wonder why we never just wheeled it into the open for all the world to see!

Another church-goer's secret we discovered by accident: walking our friend home along that same road one night, flashing our torch about, we got an unexpected response from a croft on the opposite hill. Between the road where we walked and the croft was a deep gully which left a clear line of vision between the two points. Many times after when we walked that road flashing our torch we got a reply from a lantern in the croft byre! Poor man, we must have given him many fruitless journeys, and there was one time in particular he must have cursed us with every inch of his being. We had enjoyed our signalling session and gone home to bed when the heavens opened. The rain splattered like bullets on the shed roof and the thunder and lightning roared and snaked across the sky. My sister and I lay in bed alternating between fits of the giggles and pangs of remorse at what we had done to the poor soul!

PEARL PAUL

Summer Visitors

Each summer for six years from 1923 to 1928 my father rented a farmhouse for a month at East Kincraigie Lumphanan.

It was a mixed farm with arable crops and a variety of livestock. In the early years we travelled to Lumphanan from Aberdeen by train, the first occasion being the last summer of the Great North of Scotland Railway which became part of the London & North Eastern Railway in the amalgamation of the railway companies later that year. The station-master, Mr Marr, received us off the train with a great welcome and we were driven to the farm in one of the two cars which were plied for hire in the village. One hirer was Mr Jamieson—our favourite, because his car was a tourer and the hood folded down in fine weather. The other hirer was Mr Cadger who had a boxed saloon. He was a stern gentleman while Mr Jamieson was more jolly.

I was five years old that first summer so naturally it's the events of later years that I remember best. My brother James was three and a half years younger than I was, and the first thing we did on arrival at the farm was to visit the garden which was surrounded by a hedge and by trees which usually contained a few birds' nests. The borders were separated from each other by a low box hedge and there was a large number of blackcurrant bushes to which I shall refer later. At the front door there was a porch where we could sit. My mother had been brought up on a farm near Huntly so she loved the freedom of rural life: father provided a swing which was fixed up between two trees and was a source of much enjoyment.

The sitting room, which was down a few steps from the kitchen, was furnished with a round mahogany table where we had our meals. The settee and chairs were stuffed with horse hair and covered in black material. On wet days this room was where we sat and listened to father reading to us from Charles Dickens: off it was a small bedroom where I slept. The other bedrooms were upstairs and each was provided with a porcelain basin and ewer to match. (One of us once broke a ewer and an exact replacement was eventually found in a second-hand shop in Aberdeen.) There was no inside toilet and the privy was a wooden hut outside the garden. It had a small window in the door through which we had a view of the hills to the south and of the stream trains as they ran between Lumphanan and Dess.

There was a wood of fir trees about half a mile away where we picked blaeberries which made our tongues blue: some were made into jam to take home. The fir cones were also an attraction.

Near the wood was a cottage occupied by a Miss Kemp. Her garden was a great source of pleasure to us as she grew strawberries which she generously shared with visitors passing by. I can still smell the scent of the honeysuckle and Sweet Williams which flourished there. Wild flowers grew in profusion along the roadsides—yellow broom, bluebells, white yarrow and caroldoddies which we used to fight with to see which head would be knocked off first.

There were two or three farm servants who lived in the chaumer and took their meals in the kitchen. The work on the farm was always interesting. At the haymaking we sat on top of the coles as they were dragged by a horse to where they were built into rucks or stacks. The servant lass brought tea and jam pieces to the field at the morning and afternoon breaks. At the end of the day we rode on the horses' backs as they returned to the stable. The cows were brought in to the byre twice a day to be milked by hand. We didn't like the milk fresh from the cow but preferred it cold. There were pigs in a sty, and I can still hear the squeals when they were scrubbed and washed the night before being taken to the mart at Alford to be sold. Hens, cocks, turkeys, geese and ducks roamed about the farmyard. The method which Mrs Dunn used to kill a hen for the pot was quite simple. In an outhouse with a stone floor she held the fowl upside down, placing a metal poker on the floor across its neck and her feet on each end of the poker. She then broke its neck by pulling its legs upward!

Our neighbour Mr Dunn had a ferret which he kept in a hutch with a wire-mesh door, and I sometimes accompanied him to the hill with the ferret and his gun. He put the ferret down a rabbit hole to drive out the rabbits which he then shot for the pot, but on one occasion a baby rabbit ran out and Mr Dunn caught it and gave it to me as a pet. Needless to say it did not survive.

There were two churches at Lumphanan. The parish church was half-a-mile west of the village and the minister was Mr Donald. We usually went to the United Free Church were Mr Lawson was minister. It was on the north side of the village and further away for us to walk. One Sunday in the parish church it got very dark as the sky had become overcast, and the beadle decided that the minister could do with some light to see his sermon which he was in the course of delivering. There was a paraffin lamp on each side of the pulpit, and the beadle went forward, lifted one lamp out of its socket, shook it, and finding it contained no oil proceeded to the other lamp and duly lit it. All the while Mr Donald continued with his sermon as if nothing had happened.

Charlie Dunn did not attend church regularly. His Sunday ritual was to walk up to the road-end at 10 a.m. where he was joined by his neighbours Mr King of Knappyround and Mr Stewart of Quithelhead. There they stood, leaning on the fence, no doubt discussing the state of the crops, livestock prices and other weighty matters (probably including their summer visitors). On the Lammas term day Mr Dunn would put on his best suit and proceed along with his neighbours to the Macbeth Arms Hotel beside the railway station, where the Estate Factor would be waiting to collect the rent from them. They were rewarded with a dram or sometimes a free lunch.

Father had only two weeks holiday and during the rest of the month he travelled daily by train to Aberdeen. The first train in the morning from Ballater was the express which only stopped at Aboyne and at Torphins where he joined it. He cycled there and the station staff put his cycle on a train to Lumphanan during the day where it awaited his return in the evening!

My grandfather, Alexander Gill, was in his eighties at this time (he lived on to the age of 94) and used to join us for part of the holiday. He had a watchmaker's business in Aberdeen, and as he became friendly with some of the folk in the area he often repaired their clocks.

One visit he used to make was to a Mr Cromar who had a small farm at Milltown near the railway crossing alongside the road to Dess, and when the King travelled to Balmoral we went to those crossgates to see the royal train go past. In those days the coaches were painted white. It was quite a sight. There were no ordinary trains on Sundays until 1928, but each Sunday when the King was in residence at Balmoral an engine with one carriage passed on its way to Ballater carrying the King's mail!

One Sunday my brother James complained of stomach pains and my father hired Mr Cadger to run us over to Dess where our doctor's wife, also a doctor, was on holiday. She thought James might have appendicitis and recommended taking him to Aberdeen to consult her husband.

It being Sunday with no public transport Mr Cadger took James, accompanied by our mother and father, into town. The doctor was cautious and kept the patient under observation for a day or two, but the trouble cleared up and they returned to rejoin me at the end of the week. That was when James confessed to having drunk water from the trough while playing at horses. My father always complained that it was a very expensive drink!

MORRISON GILL

The Berry Market: Cornhill

Preparations for the Berry Market began a few days before the due date, when gipsy caravans came into the park across from my grandmother's cottage. The market had two purposes, one being togather a crowd who would buy all the surplus gooseberries, raspberries and strawberries, and the other to meet up with and engage extra men for the corn harvest. A marquee was put up in the park and folk fae a' the airts cam' in aboot for a dance on the evening before the market began.

We children were called into the house and could only look through the windows. Flush-faced men strutted and reeled about in great good humour after visiting the pub or its 'annexe' at the park gate.

Folk were bringing in fruit by the cart load and some of the tinker's 'stannies' were already doing business. Stalls were being erected, and Biddell's Amusements had a Shooting Gallery and four Showdy (swing) Boats which were already in operation. We could hardly wait for our parents to come the next day, as fairs need money!

As soon as the Rudge-Multi stopped at the back door next day, Bill and I tugged our parents over the road to get pokes of candy—cinnamon, clove, hoarhound and peppermint—at Candy Nellie's stand, and a big bag of green peas-in-the-pod, and another of strawberries, at different stalls. My money was going done when I noticed a local baker's stall with miniature currant loaves and biscuits shaped like gingerbread mannies. I had kept sixpence to buy something from my two Grandmas, but the jewellery stall had no suitable thimbles or trinkets so I decided to give them currant loaves and to spend the tuppence left on a turn on the Showdy Boat. How I wished I hadn't! It soared up and plunged down and I had to hold on for grim death—and when others squealed with delight I couldn't utter a squeak. I thought it would never stop, but when it did, I managed a wan smile and told everybody I liked it fine!

LAURA WILSON

Sabbath Evening

When the Sunday dishes were put back in the cupboard, my grandfather sat down in the big armchair: he had been a tall man when young but now he was bent almost double by the hard work of breaking in the land. My grandmother fetched the enormous Family Bible and placed it on his knee, and then she sat in the smaller high chair while my brother and I brought forward stoods and sat between. I can see grandpa still, bald, bearded like a prophet in the Bible, bending over a page which had a blue place-marker on it. My little grandmother sat straight up in her prim high-necked black dress. She wore a black jet mourning-brooch in which was set a plaited lock of the hair of her youngest child, Georgie, who had died of diphtheria when he was three and was still mourned by his mother. She lowered her eyes and crossed her hands on her lap.

Grandpa began to read in a deep sonorous voice. The words didn't mean much to me but the reverence and solemnity were hypnotic. For the first ten minutes my eyes never left his face—but then my gaze moved to the fire where fascinating shapes appeared and flickered and changed and disappeared so that I hardly noticed that the reading had turned into prayer until my grandma whispered, "Kneel down, lass". This was far from comfortable and I got restless, examining the knees of my white cotton crocheted Sunday stockings and changing to sitting on my bottom instead.

Soon after that, grandpa struck the key on the tuning fork and launched into a Psalm in the slow, scoopy fashion that he had used when he led the singing in the Church. Grandma had a thin, quavery soprano voice and also scooped up from one note to the next. I didn't know the words but I sang the alto harmony in sol-fa just as I had heard my mother do at choir practices and musical evenings in our home, except that I adopted the slow speed and 'scoop'. Then we all managed to take part in 'The Lord's Prayer' which brought the service to an end.

There was a quiet pause, after which grandpa closed the Bible and grandma carefully put it back on the parlour table. Then she proceeded to unfasten the 'dickey'—a sort of stiff, white collar with a bit which tucked under his jacket revers which grandpa wore on Sundays. Grandpa then wound up the Grandfather Clock and consulted his big, silver pocketwatch.

"Noo bairns ye'd better be off to bed."

LAURA WILSON

Memories of Cullen

The long night's journey had delivered us at Aberdeen, the coast train had arrived at Cullen, and a hired pony and trap awaited us and our luggage. Five miles of up and down road now—would the pony manage the steep Manse brae? She did, and now, along the back of the wood, round the corner, and down at the end of the sloping field, was the Croft.

The pony stepped carefully down the track which led from the head of the road to the green where Aunt Jeannie waited to greet us. We children had little time or patience for emotional greetings—were there any calfies in the byre? any clucking hens? any baby chickens?

The promise of food drew us into the house; oatcakes, girdle scones and tea kept us busy while the grown-ups called the roll of friends and relations—who was away to Australia or Canada—who had given up or taken on a croft? and who was awa' deid?

The First World War had brought many changes and some improvements. The thatched roof of the house had been replaced by slates, with two attic bedrooms added. In the kitchen, the wall bed was now enclosed behind wooden doors which stretched from floor to ceiling. Upstairs, our bedroom was simply furnished—one bed for mother and youngest child, mattresses on the floor for others, a jug of water, a basin, and skylights in the roof—perfect! There was only one snag: the 'wee hoose' was at some distance. But needs must, and there was a lovely, if draughty view.

There was no water laid on in the house—it all had to be drawn at the well, brought in in pails, and stored in the water hole in the passage. The occasional bath was therefore an event of some importance when the kitchen was vacated and the water heated on the fire, and poured into a small tin bath wherein the chosen victim was inserted and duly scrubbed.

The Sabbath was a day of great solemnity and reverence. In the Room, whose only function was to house articles of prime importance, Grand Uncle's Sabbath claes were laid out, brushed, put on, brushed again. We were lined up for inspection, and having passed muster, away we went in slow and steady marching step, over the green, through the wood, and down the brae to the kirk, where the bell was giving out the final warning.

The minister's wife was already in her place, her feather boa about her neck, a veil securing her hat tied under her chin. The minister's daughter played the harmonium powerfully and sang with equal power joined by those young ladies of the choir whose hats and hair styles would survive the effort. It was very hot; through our thin dresses we stuck to the recently varnished pews and care was needed in detaching ourselves. But at last, the service with its long sermon was over; greetings were exchanged, visits promised, and away we went under the scorching sun.

Only necessary works could be performed on the Sabbath—feeding animals and humans, milking the cows, and fetching water to fill pails—but hearing that 'the folk f'ae Lunnon are hame', neighbours would call in for a 'news' and as soon as possible we children would escape to the wood cool and green whose silence beat upon the ear.

Not only on the Sabbath, but every day, the back of the wood was my favourite place for sitting. The hills of Gamrie, away in the distance, closed in the landscape; in another direction a streak of deep blue was the sea, where one day we might go. The heavy clop-clop of horses' hooves foretold the arrival of a peat-laden cart going home from the moss, horse and man tormented by flies.

In the depths of the wood, all was enchantment: softest green moss in which feet sank to ankle depth, purple heather, and sometimes a sprig of white. A swampy patch was known as Meg's Loch—why? we wondered but never found out, explanations differing widely. Blaeberries were abundant, their juice indelible on pinafores.

We didn't realise at that time the sacrifice Aunt Jean had made in lending us her bicycle, the sole means of transport. A grown-up cousin patiently instructed us, turn about, and later, with more borrowing of bicycles, conducted us far and wide over the countryside and even as far as the sea.

Delights abounded: we loved to watch Aunt Jean milking—"Haud still ye fashous cratur"—to smell the byre smell, to hear the angry squawk of a thwarted hen. The baker came right down to the green with his cairtie; the fishwife brought fish caught only hours before; the postie came with letters and news, going on his way refreshed by a cuppie o' tea.

Rainy days were particularly delightful, for up the stair was a landing with a cupboard full of books and old magazines, all of which we read assiduously, ears cocked for the next call to food. It had to end—we knew that—but next year, ah, 'next year' already gleamed bright on the horizon and if all were spared and well, we would be back!

EVELYN RAFFAN

Scared

Sitting with our cold feet near the fire had one draw-back—it produced chilblains, which were the bane of our lives every winter. There was only one remedy. Every night, before bed-time, the little green cake of 'Snow-fire' was put on a saucer and placed on the bink to soften. Then, one by one, we rubbed our chilblained toes, the menthol fragrance filling our nostrils as the soft greasiness eased the burning, itching ache. Meanwhile the pan of milk, also heated on the bink, made our supper-time cocoa—then it was off to bed.

That was when the fire ceased being my friend. My little sister and I shared a small bed in the corner of the living-room. When the gas-lamp was turned out and everyone was in bed, the embers of the fire still glowed, every now and then leaping into flames as a draught stirred them to life. The shadows they cast became little devils with horns and forked tails, and monsters with scaly backs, which climbed up the walls and along the roof. Crook-backed witches, with straggly hair, stretched out long scraggy fingers ever nearer and nearer—even up over the bed-clothes. As the flames died they disappeared, but I could hear them still, cackling and sighing, as the furniture, doors and window-frames contracted in the cooling room!

WILMA FAID

The Baker

Motor vehicles were few and far between. The horses that pulled carts were all docile plodding creatures, their pace determined mainly by the fact that they might otherwise miss the 'shaves' of loaf and jam proffered so generously by small grubby hands.

The baker's horse was large and brown, as was his van. I can still recall the wonderful aroma of fresh bread that wafted out when he opened the doors, and how he would present me with a 'sair-heidie'—a round sponge-cake topped with icing the exact colour and consistency of 'Germolene' ointment, and completely surrounded by a bandage of grease-proof paper.

BARBARA BANKS

Hogmanay

Suitably wrapped against the cold and armed with the customary brown paper carrier bag, (which was invariably sodden and disintegrated before you reached the second house) various bands of youngsters set off. The nearest I've come to discovering something similar is Hallowe'en, though in our village Hallowe'en was considered begging. Hogmanay was, however, a different matter.

All the adults of the village seemed to accept the fact that at some point during the run up to the bells, a motley band would appear at their door chanting,

> Rise up good wives and shak' yer feathers,
> Dinna think that we are beggars,
> We're only good bairnies come oot tae play,
> So rise up and gies oor Hogmanay.
> A cogie fu' of brandy, a cogie fu' of beer,
> We wish ye, we bless, ye, A Happy New Year.

This was usually followed by a chant of 'Three o' us' or whatever which I presume was a way of warning the inhabitants of the various houses about how much money, how many tangerines, or how many glasses of cordial they would have to give out. Some people made you do further party pieces inside the house for your bit of black bun while others hurriedly handed you tuppence or thruppence, probably just to shut you up. Whatever the reason, no adult ever refused, no matter the circumstances. Even the poor souls we tormented on and off for the rest of the year obliged with a cup of cordial or a bit of black bun! The fact that we rarely got to sing the second verse on the doorstep speaks volumes!

J McLEISH

Going to School: Glenlivet

I started school in Glenlivet in 1922. I don't know how much I learned, but the road there and back was filled with interest. There were snails creeping about in the ditch at the side of the road that were black and sticky and if I touched them they pulled in their 'horns' and grew smaller. I can still see the burn with its mimulus or 'mappie's mous' in large yellow clumps and watery wagtails tripping and bobbing amongst the stones at the water's edge.

Just before the road went through the wood there was a very tall old tree which I thought might fall on me so I always ran at speed past it. Beyond the wood on the bank at the side of the road going down to the smiddy, wild rose bushes grew. I always looked in at the door of the smiddy to see the huge fire and the horses getting their shoes hammered on. Down the brae from the school, on the bank amongst the trees was a big smooth flat rock sloping down into the wood at the side of the river Livet. We called it the slidey stane, and one night after school I had a wonderful time on it. I'd on navy blue knickers and black knitted stockings and I must have looked a sight when I got home! I don't think I had any seat left in my knickers and I certainly didn't have any knees left on my stockings—I remember struggling hard to conceal the gaping holes!

ANNE E SHAW

Truant

It was 1912 and The Turra Coo was to be sold at 2 p.m. by Public Auction in The Square, Turriff, so quite a number of us decided that we would attend the sale instead of school. The Janitor was sent to bring us back but we hid amongst the farmers and farm servants and he couldn't find us. He was an ex-Navy man of a rather fiery temper, and as he was jostled by the crowd, his face became redder and redder and his little pill box hat more askew. He returned to school empty-handed, but, when we did eventually reach our classrooms the Headmaster punished the boys with the tawse and told the girls that he would write to their parents saying that their bursaries would be stopped! I had £5 a year for cycle maintenance and for a time I went home in fear and trembling, lest a letter should have arrived; but none ever came and my parents never found out!

BARBARA J WATSON

Free Boots

Oft time I view my childhood days
Through years that bridge the gap
An' see again my parish boots
Wi' the twa holes at the tap

The parish mannie o' that time
Wid lang be deid an' gone
But swear I will that pair o' boots
Could still be hangin' on

For weel I mind he says tae me
'They'll last ye a' yer life
An' serve ye good an' be tae you
as faithful as a wife.'

They gave tae me a lift that day
An' took me aff the grun
Wi' near three hunner tackets
An' they felt like half a ton

But oh! boy they were beezers
An' I'd wait 'til it wis dark
Ta skite them on the causie steens
An' thrill tae see the spark

Ye can speak o' faithful servants
Wha wid come tae your defence
Well those that felt the force o' them
Wid nae hae sit doon since

The toffs' kids had a swagger
Wi' their cricket bat an' cap
An' they'd snub me 'cause I'd parish boots
Wi' twa holes at the tap

But nae doot there's some amongst them
Finished up much worse than me
An' would gladly trade their high horse
For a pair o' boots that's free.

DOUGLAS BARBER

Into Service

March 1928, and next month I would have my fourteenth birthday and would be leaving the village school in June.

During the past year I had followed in turn, my sister Annie, and then brother Jimmy, and gone to work on Saturdays, and school holidays, with a Miss McLean at a croft near the sea on the Moray Firth.

Miss McLean was Highland and a beautiful speaker. She was housekeeper to the two Mr Duncans who had owned the croft and also contracted to collect the salmon caught by the netting crews all along the Spey. The fish were kept in long wooden boxes and collected morning and evening and taken to the Salmon Station to be measured, weighed, packed in ice, labelled, and driven to the railway station for dispatch in the guard's van, for the London market.

Miss McLean was an excellent cook and baker, and had orders for oatcakes, scones and cakes from the nearby hotel and houses let out to summer visitors. My favourite duty was to deliver such orders as I'd very often get a 'tip' of tuppence, or maybe even sixpence! Usually most of my Saturday was taken up with washing dishes, milk pails and utensils, paring tatties and cleaning vegetables. No cash payment, but a basket packed with all kinds of groceries, and an added bonus at Christmas time of large fruit cake, shortbread, a tin of assorted mixed cream biscuits, apples, oranges and a bottle of Port wine. Two of us were needed to carry home such generous and welcome gifts and we were only too happy to work for this really kind and friendly lady.

Nearing April, one Saturday, Miss McLean casually asked if I'd care to go to work at 'The Bungalow'. This was owned by a wealthy family in Keith, and was kept open all year round by a housekeeper and young maid.

During the following week a white-haired gentleman visited our school whom we took to be an Inspector. He doffed his hat when he came through the door and nodded around the class, and then he and the Headmaster spoke together in earnest conversation.

The next Saturday Miss McLean told me that I had to be at the Bungalow on the Tuesday at 4 p.m. to be 'interviewed' by Mr K.

When I got home I told this to my eldest sister Maggie who had kept house for father and the family still at school since our Mam had died when I was newly five, the youngest of the family of seven—six girls and one boy. Maggie pondered what I could wear for this important occasion in my life. My pal Lily and I set off walking on Sunday to the Braes of Engie farm, where Elsie, another sister, was Cook. I delivered a note to her from Maggie asking it I might borrow her heather mixture jumper and skirt.

Elsie gave us tea and scones in the kitchen, parcelled up the garments and wished me good luck for the interview.

Tuesday came at last and I cycled staight from school to the Bungalow. A large maroon-coloured, straight-backed car sat outside the gate. I leaned my bike against the railings and walked to the back door. Helen, the maid, brought me into the kitchen and introduced me to the housekeeper and then opened a door into a long corridor covered in brown lino with a Greek Key pattern border. There were doors on both sides. Helen tapped on the farthest door from the kitchen and was told "Come in", so she opened this door and showed me into a sitting room.

The gentleman who had come to school was sitting there and he invited me to walk over near him—I can't recall if I was asked to sit down, but rather think I stood in front of him while he asked questions. "What did I know about housework?" When I didn't know how to answer, he helped out by saying the Headmaster and Miss McLean had assured him that I was quick and willing to learn. Then, did I understand about being honest? Yes. This gave no trouble as we had been brought up in a very honest and caring family.

Next he took me all through the rooms—the dining room directly opposite the sitting room and located near the front door; four bedrooms simply furnished, with lino covered floors and rugs. The bathroom and separate W.C. were in the centre of the lobby, and in a recess a long table with an upright telephone—the first telephone I'd ever seen!

In the back regions there was a place for coal, firewood and brushes. A store room with shelves of tins of all kinds also held large glass dishes which I later found contained tongue, brawn, boar's head and tins of fruit. There were also racks for fruit and vegetables. Next was the scullery with a sink and a three-burner paraffin cooker with a tin oven to set on top. From there a door went outside to the coal shed and the drying green.

Inside again was a large sun parlour furnished with basket chairs, with shelves all round the glass windows full of flowering plants in pots. Next was the maid's bedroom divided by a coloured curtain into a large part for the housekeeper, and a much smaller part for the maid. I trembled with embarrassment as the beds were unmade and Mr K said "If you come here see that this doesn't occur." He opened the door into the kitchen and said to the maid "See that Jessie gets a cup of tea." I felt like hiding. None-the-less the two ladies didn't appear in the least put out and we all chatted away together. When I collected the cups into the sink to wash them, Helen tittered and said "I think you'd be best to use the basin".

I felt mortified as I couldn't understand anyone using a basin (which I had to do at home) when there was a sink.

One evening soon after someone went past the window at home and Maggie, in answer to her query "Is this were Jessie Minty lives?" invited her in. A formidable looking lady with a big black and white dog on a lead came in. She was dressed in a knitted cardigan suit with woollen hat to match, brown flat shoes and diamond-patterned woollen stockings.

She looked all around—at the wide open chimney fireplace with the small bunks and the steel fender with the oval brass inset 'HOME SWEET HOME'; at the box bed in the opposite wall with its red Paisley patterned curtains; at the table under the window with the oilcloth cover; and at the little table with its fringed red cover and the American clock on top, and Father's melodion. There were home made clootie rugs on the floor and, hanging at Father's side of the fire, the net which he was in the process of weaving for the fishing. She was very taken up with this home employment and the fact that all the tools were hand-made by Father, and I had to demonstrate filling a needle with twine. Another thing she wanted to know was if the treadle sewing machine was used. Yes—all our clothes were made on it by Maggie—not only for the family, but for neighbours as well. She then breezed away with her dog in her chauffeur-driven car.

Saturday came again with a message from Miss McLean that I had to be at the Bungalow on the following Tuesday. I was met with friendly smiles: Mrs K thought I'd be suitable, and I'd be provided with uniform and a wage of £2.10s. per month! I could hardly take in all this good news. I was to report on the 28th May, although they understood I'd have to attend school until two weeks into June. Miss Sim, the new housekeeper, would also be starting on the 'term day' 28th May, and the car was to collect her from her home in Elgin.

Great excitement and preparations! Maggie and I went to Bonnyman's the drapers shop in Portgordon where we bought two Vedonis vests and two pairs of lockknit knickers, two pairs of black lisle stockings and one pair of black 'house shoes' with flat heels and an ankle-strap with button tie.

My sister Helen gave me a toothbrush, a tin of Gibb's Dentrifrice, and soap in a waterproof bag. Elsie gave me a grey cardigan, and also a strawberry-red hat with a high crown and narrow brim which was fashionable then. I also had a case for my belongings—it was strong cardboard, grained like crocodile skin with two locks, two keys and a tin handle.

I came home from school on the afternoon of the 28th all nerves and excitement as the chauffeur was to collect me. When we arrived at the

Bungalow Miss Sim the new housekeeper was already there and Mr K introduced us, but he very soon left and we began to get acquainted. Miss Sim was old I thought, with white hair in a small bun at the back, dressed in blouse, black skirt and white tea apron. She was tall and angular but obviously a nice person.

We went through to our bedroom and there laid out on my bed was the promised uniform—a grey Alpaca dress with lined bodice, buttoning down the front to the waist. This was to be worn in the afternoon with a small fancy 'tea' apron in white cotton, along with a cap, trimmed with black velvet ribbon threaded through slits. Two blue cotton dresses were for morning wear—much the same style as the grey one, but worn with a full-sized white apron with bib and crossed straps at the back and a Sister Dora cap which had a deep off-the-face cuff. I had to try the dresses on, and felt gauche and awkward. Miss Sim said I didn't need to wear uniform unless any of the family were staying.

She showed me how to spread a tea cloth on the end of the big kitchen table, and how to set out the cups, knives and forks in the proper way. I observed carefully and I daresay I did need more than one telling, or showing, of the way to do certain jobs.

We sat by a lovely fire in the kitchen and at nine o'clock I took the milk pail and crossed the green for the milk from Miss McLean. She quizzed me about how things were shaping and I told her all about my first day.

Next morning I got up at seven-thirty, dressed for school, and went out and filled the coal scuttle and a box of kindling sticks. The table was set for breakfast and I was asked if I wanted bacon and egg, or porridge. I was shy to ask for bacon and egg as we never had that at home, and so sat down to a large half of a yellowish orange and did what Miss Sim did—sprinkled caster sugar over it and cut out segments with a pointed spoon. It was delicious—my first grapefruit! Porridge, toast and marmalade followed—all luxury. I cleared the table and washed the dishes and put everything away in their places. Miss Sim came to the door to see me away on my bike, to school. What boasting and showing off to the girls in my class, telling about uniforms, grapefruit and so on.

When I returned at three-thirty the car was sitting at the gate so I knew either Mrs or Mr K was down—never both. I hurriedly changed into afternoon uniform and soft house shoes, and was shown how to set a tea tray and also a three-tiered cake stand. I carried the tray carefully through the long corridor, tapped at the sitting room door and entered when told. I'd been instructed by Miss Sim that when I answered I'd add "M-M" to Yes or No to Mrs K and "Sir" to Mr K. Mrs K was sitting in an armchair, and indicated that I should set the tray down on a low table close to her chair. Next I fetched in the cake stand and she spoke kindly hoping I'd be happy there.

After tea Miss Sim said I could go home for the evening but must be back by 9 p.m. to go for the milk. I sang all the way up the muir and took delight in recounting all the doings to Father and Maggie.

JESSIE STEWART

The Circus

It was an exciting day when the Circus passed on its way from Inverurie to Peterhead. The house door which normally stood open, was closed and locked, and I watched the procession from the kitchen window. The vans were all horse-drawn, the heavier requiring two horses. The elephants walked. I was afraid to go out of doors as my mother had told me the story of little Freddie Charlesworth who was kidnapped by the circus people and his parents didn't find him for many years after. I was afraid that I too might be kidnapped if I went outside. . . .

BARBARA J WATSON

Out to Play

When we played Hide and Seek, great store was set on the boundaries involved, and after much discussion, argument, and the odd case of fisticuffs, the boundaries were almost always set as the North Pole, the South Pole, Oban and Peterhead. When Winkle and Stillie, the only 18-year-olds who would condescend to play with us, used to hide, they simply disappeared to the only pub in the village and we were left the entire night looking for them.

British Bulldog was invariably played under a street lamp. The fact that it was in front of some poor woman's home did not deter us. When the noise got too much, she simply sent for the bobbies. Looking back, this must have been a feat in itself as she didn't have the 'phone. Anyway the bobbies would duly turn up and we would scatter over any available dyke, to swear revenge on the poor soul. And revenge we had in our own childish way. We would tie black thread to her door knocker, hide behind some other poor soul's hedge and pull the cord.

Long summer nights were spent playing down the shore when we couldn't cajole enough people to play anything else. We even had a built-in swimming pool among the rocks. Cold and deep, but it sufficed as a swimming pool. Funny how you don't feel the cold so much when you're young. Occasionally, we'd pull the crab boxes up and filch a partan. Driftwood and litter were collected and we'd boil the poor beastie. We didn't look on it as stealing, simply collecting the commission for selling them to the 'tourists', that is, the folk frae Torry who graced our domain in the Summer.

J McLEISH

A Mechanical Monster

Transport in my childhood was negligible; feet were the best way of getting anywhere. The lorryman's horse occupied the main streets on the daily round, but if a child was playing nearby, there would be a warning shout "Mind that bairn frae the horse!" Cars were unknown, and I well remember hearing the arrival of the first one. A woman was scrubbing her doorstep, and hearing an unusual sound, she looked up, jumped from her humble position on her knees, upset the bucket of water, and ran indoors shouting "There something comin' doon the road withoot naething!"

GAVIN THOM

THE SEA

Jist Sittin'

Sittin' here waitin', mornin' sun risin',
Yawls are acomin' through the dawn's glow.
Tubs are a'teemin', guttin' knives gleemin',
Fingers a' bandaged an' ready tae go.

Sittin' here guttin', cleanin' an' washin',
Haddocks an' fitin's score aifter score.
Haud on the salt quine, bree aff the weet brine,
Speldins are best if they're dry tae the core.

Sittin' here reddin', cleanin' an' shreddin',
Ca'n' oot tippens an' hooks in a snorl.
Strings aifter strings lie ilk in their ain wye,
Mony wints tae tie, horsehair atwirl.

Sittin' here baitin', yawls are a'waitin',
Evenin' sun startin' tae dip in the west.
Lay the line's neatly, let them rin fleetly,
Mak sure that oor yawl taks hame the best.

LEWIS MACKIE

A Day in the Life of a Fisherwoman

When Betsy woke up it was still dark outside, but she rose and lighted a taper from the still-smouldering peat in the hearth. She checked the time. It was four a.m., so she lit the paraffin lamp, pokered the peat into a blaze, then added some fresh divots, remembering first to remove the tentered fish which had been smoking overnight above the long low fire.

She stirred the oatmeal which had been 'steeped' the previous evening, and hung the pot, by its hooped handle, on the trivet over the peat, which was now properly alight.

It was time now to have a quick wash in cold water and get dressed before waking the rest of the household. She donned long flannel pantaloons over a hand-knitted vest. Next came a couple of warm, striped petticoats, which came down to her ankles. She completed her toilet with a grey blouse, and a heavy, black serge skirt. Her black hair was brushed back into a tight bun on the nape of her neck.

Her husband was awake now, and soon he too was dressed.

After their breakfast of porridge with a plentiful helping of milk he went off to get his yawl ready for the day's fishing. It was more of a coble really, not having an engine, but did boast a small mast and a sail.

It was rowed out to the fishing just beyond the bar in the Aberdeen Harbour. Being inshore fishermen, John and his partner had to fish within a three mile limit, so they would row out, shoot their lines, haul them back in after a short spell and then make their way to Aberdeen Market to sell some of their catch.

With her husband off to work Betsy now got her bairns up and attended to their breakfast. She had two girls and a boy. John, the youngest, was named after his father, which was the custom among the fisher folk. The eldest girl, Betty, was named after her mother, while Maggie, the younger sister, was called after her mother's sister.

They too had their chores to do before going to school, and after seeing they were all in order Betsy put her smoked fish into a creel and changed her hand-knitted woollen moggins for a sturdy pair of tackety boots. She then threw a grey shawl over her shoulders, and put a clean white apron and the lapbag she had made to hold the proceeds of her fish sales, into her murlin, which she carried in the crook of her arm.

Slipping her arms through the cords at each side, she put the creel on her back; then, picking up her murlin and giving last-minute instructions to the children, she set off on the four-mile journey from Cove Bay to Aberdeen.

She walked along briskly down by Burnbanks, cutting across from there to Nigg Brae and then down past the New St Fitticks Kirk and on to the shore where she boarded the Ferry for the Aberdeen side of the River Dee.

Once across, her first port of call was the Fish Market, where she would buy a ling, and a few small haddock or whiting.

A rather small, square room which the fisher girls called the Glass-house was furnished with some wooden tables and scales. Betsy found a place to fillet the ling she had bought, and weighed it into half pound or one pound pieces. The fisher women used their own knives for this purpose.

While the women worked they exchanged news and views, but everyone was in a hurry, aiming to be the first at the Green to secure a favourite stance. Each had her own special customers, and they would chat about each other's families, and other items of interest.

If there was any fish left as the afternoon wore on, Betsy would walk to the town, where her favourite vending places were the Shiprow, the Guestrow, and the Castlegate end of Union Street, where gentry and rich merchants still lived, although the West End of Union Street was now considered very upper-class.

She didn't stay long as she liked to be home for the main meal in the evening.

She made her way back to Cove Bay, crossing the Ferry again for a few pennies. Her money by this time had been transferred into a strong pouch bag, tied securely with a string across its mouth, and placed in the bottom of her creel. She didn't walk quite so briskly on the way home as it was mostly uphill, but eventually she arrived.

The girls had got the kettle on the boil, and she brandered some of her unsold fish over the peaty fire. Anyone who hasn't tasted peat-brandered haddock has missed out on a treat!

Now you would think Betsy would be finished for the day, but this wasn't so. There was a basket of mussels which John junior had helped his father raise form the sea at the sides of the small Cove pier. The eldest girl, Betty, sheild the mussels into a pail, while her younger sister, Maggie, attended to the dishes, and did some darning.

Betsy baited the line which her husband had 'redded' earlier, cleaning and replacing any broken hooks, and untangling any ravelled bits. She coiled the line at the bottom of the scull and arranged the hooks neatly in rows at the other end, putting strips of newspaper between each row.

Any fish left over from the day's catch were cleaned and tentered and hung over the peat fire to be smoked by next morning. The peats were generously sprinkled with sawdust to encourage the fragrant peat smoke to rise: once the oatmeal was steeped for next morning's breakfast it would be time for bed.

E FINLAYSON

Collieston: Early Morning

The sea's the village heart, the vital core,
An ever-moving backdrop to the scene,
Stilled, from white breakers of the night before
To wavelets of a calm translucent green,
Stirring and plashing, gently, on the shore.

The sunrise touches windowpane and wall,
Lightly slowly spreads to Ness, and boats, and beach,
Shade and cool greenness where rock shadows fall,
Rippled reflection where the rock pools reach,
Till the warm glow of morning colours all.

And sometimes, as I wake, I think I hear
Soft, through the raucous cry of circling gull,
The measured tread of rubber boot on pier,
The thunk of oar in rowlock, rope on hull,
The well-remembered sounds of yesteryear.

M WILLIAMSON

Fisher Quines

The year was 1930 and I was seventeen. Jobs for young girls were very scarce around Banff so along with my friends I joined the band of Scottish Fisher Lassies who gutted, packed and salted for curing the herring which were shipped in their thousands to the Continent. It was the time of the herring boom in the North Sea and we were part of it. I remember putting stencils on the bottom of the barrels for all the different ports of destination. Danzig still sticks in my mind.

We chose to start at Wick in Caithness and we went there in the first days of June. The weather was very good that year and we had plenty of work. There were twelve crews of girls, two crews from the North East of Scotland and ten crews of girls from the outer isles of the West coast. They could all speak and understand our 'English' but preferred to speak Gaelic. We worked very well together and they soon had us singing in their language. The crews from the West coast lived in huts provided by the fish buyers, but we lived in 'The Cabin'. This was a deck cabin off a ship washed ashore near Wick which had been taken up to a lovely grassy site overlooking Wick Harbour. We were very comfortable there with a stove, living space and two bedrooms.

MARY B FINDLAY

Novelties

On the platorm at York on our way to Yarmouth, there were boys selling chocolate and sweets, and also some things we had never seen before which cost two old pennies a bag. We were nosey and bought a bag each. They were really different and very tasty but when we were finished eating them there was a small blue paper still left in the bag and we couldn't imagine what it could be. It was of course salt and that was our very first taste of tattie crisps!

MARY B FINDLAY

Pebble, Stone and Shell

We walked to the beach,
silver sands empty
of distracting life.
She wanted to talk
but her words
fell short of my hearing,
lost in the gentle sound
of lapping waves.
Bathed
in the warmth of the sun
I removed my shoes,
felt the cooling sand
measure and shape
my footprints
in loving embrace.
She handed me a pebble,
smoothed and glazed,
polished
by passing time
but
needing water
to refract its beauty.
She talked
as I mused on this
contrary friend,
the sea.

She selected a stone
at her feet,
pointed and sharp
to the touch
glistening as the sun
sought
its sparkling crystal hues.
I compared
the pebble's lacklustre dryness,
the stone's glittering life.
Wondrous nature
and all that she is.
I watched.
She bent down
to the gentle surf
and gave me
the object
found—
a shell,
sad and worn
its delicate fabric marred,
life
long since gone,
forces
that once gave life
now breaking down.
We ended our walk.
Looking back,
witnessed
tidal erasure of
our presence.

JAMES TAYLOR

Servant Lassie

The servant lassie was a necessity when the children were small, because
the wives of fishermen in the small villages round the coast of Scotland
were also involved almost full-time in the business of fishing. The servant
lassie was there to do the housework and look after the family. The girl
lived as part of the family; money didn't come into it—or if it did, it was

no more than a pound for a whole year. But the girl's family was spared keeping an extra daughter until time for her to marry, and she certainly earned her keep in the fisher family. Cooking, cleaning, drawing water from the communal well and washing clothes were all part of her duties. Only occasionally did the woman of the house help with the daily routine of household chores, and that was when the weather had been bad for a few days and the men could not launch their boats.

DOROTHY H MAIR

Money

Money once earned couldn't be spent immediately. You never knew when the next money would come in, so the tin box on the dresser was never allowed to be empty. The income of most of the families in the village was on a par, and a man could easily work out how much his neighbour had earned in a given time; so when a man suddenly bought a brand new boat from the boatbuilders conjecture about how he had got the money was inevitably rife. In the end the most popular idea seemed to be that his father, following the wreck of a schooner on the rocks south of the village some thirty years before, had found a leather pouch of sovereigns. This money should of course have been handed to the Wreck Commissioners, but proof that he had found it had never been forthcoming.

DOROTHY H MAIR

Acorn Days

It all began when my father, a few weeks earlier, purchased from Peterhead the Girl May's lifeboat, a twelve foot, flat-sterned open craft, proclaimed unsinkable owing to the copper tanks built into her sides. With a change in fishing trends, and the introduction of the less bulky inflatables, skippers and boat owners alike were virtually casting these expertly built life-savers into their compounds, where they lay amongst the rest of the unwanted gear—hence the price of £15.

To power the vessel, my father also purchased an outboard motor. High hopes of a quick return on our initial outlay were heightened by the seeming prosperity of the part-time mackerel and lobster fishermen who plied eidently from our small local harbour.

The long June evenings saw our boat transformed with liberal clorts of white paint, and a yellow top rail that contrasted with the bold black lettering of her name and number—*Acorn* B.F. 306. Now she lay sleek and gleaming at the top of our harbour slipway.

With mental images of the 'Big Oak' to come, I waited impatiently for the school holidays. Then, at last, the big day.

As with every local launch, an air of excitement prevailed, and an excess of volunteers left the actual owners with little to do except watch, as an overpowering force took control of the situation. Each man seemed to gain a strange uplift from helping to initiate another's vessel. Alas, as easily as these helpful crews were stimulated, they were also discouraged; and at the slightest sign of some mishap, the eager crowd could smartly turn into a pessimistic squad of deserters, each offering a different excuse, as steps were retraced from the lower end of the slipway.

"Dear me, is 'at the time?"; "A' weel, 'at's tattie time"; "Ye'll hae tae try something—she's ga'in doon", advised a third; "Ower lang oot o' the water. She's druchted!" he added with a dry air of finality, and passed a rope into my hand. Its purpose had been to pull the boat to her proper berth. We stood in silence each with a hand on the rope, and watched her slowly submerge. Low water—and the boat had listed to port. I trudged wearily across the bottom of the harbour, and, with an old bucket, baled out our shattered dream. Come the flood-tide and she was, to my amazement, WATERTIGHT, her dehydrated planks miraculously swollen to their original form. Seawater, science and nature, together or singly, had saved the day, and with faith restored, we bolted the small outboard engine to the stern and were ship-shape.

Unable to sit still I paced the kitchen floor, gorging myself with corned beef sandwiches that were a 'shove-by' till suppertime. My father was late. Of all the days, this had to be the one. A strong desire to leave him behind and go solo was dampened by the fear of starting an engine that required a stronger arm than mine to heave the starter rope.

At last, after much fussing and double checking, we left for the harbour, mackerel flies, lead weights and lines in my hand, black G.P.O. issue leggings (my father was village postman), and a tightly folded oilskin smock tucked under my arm.

"A fine nicht for 'em", said an old sea-farer, in dark gansie and trousers. He sat amongst a clique of similarly dressed gnarled seamen, who gathered most summer evenings to forecast the next day's weather and swop stories while the sun sank slowly behind the Muckle Rock. I longed to be on a par with these great men; to enthral the nautically uneducated, with bold tales of my own, of fishing boats and storms at sea, of disasters and triumphs; to speak, with idle familiarity, of far off ports and herring grounds, Shields and Lowestoft, the Isle of Man, the Minch and Mallaig. I remembered my grandfather, rock-solid, huge and hooknosed, perching me among the drying sun-baked salmon nets in the midst of his cronies, while they relived their sailing boat and drifter days in a blue haze of tobacco reek.

"A fine nicht for 'em", repeated the old man.

"Aye", I bluffed, and hoped he was right.

"Weel, i' water's nae ower thick", he volunteered and abruptly stood up. With a quick scan in the general direction we would be fishing, he dumped his backside again into the vacant concrete space.

"Nae eese if the water's thick", he repeated, and with nods and grunts of agreement from his mates this strange logic was confirmed. Completely baffled by this 'thick water' comment, I continued seawards, images of boats full of sweaty fishermen struggling with oars in a pale green sea of porridge uppermost in my mind. Due to the harbour 'drying out' the *Acorn* had been withdrawn to the relative safety of the non-tidal east breakwater some hours earlier, and the echo of the engine's exhaust bubbling at the water's edge as she dipped and bowed at her moorings, prompted me to a smarter pace.

From the top of the pier I saw my father already in his oilskins obviously eager to take up his new command. He gestured me to come down. I eyed my armful of gear, then the long vertical stepladder. I had often seen experienced men negotiate this 'one-handed', the other hand carrying (hooked on the fingers) a huge conger to be cut up for bait, or a fry of saithe, a boil of partans, assorted fishing tackle or even an engine part in need of repair. The action needed great strength and balance to heave the body in an upward swing, while the free hand made a grab for the next rung. I looked at my load, at my thin white hands, and at the long way down the rusted iron rungs: my mind floundered hopelessly for a solution, which eventually came unasked, in a long-suffering voice from my father—"Yer gear—throw it doon afore ye fa' doon—an' dinna jist drap it, be sure tae throw't". I realised I should have tried a legging first or maybe the jacket, as the two pound weight with the mackerel hooks attached almost severed my father's ear. I let the rest fall and descended the steps, ignoring the "MY God, can THIS (meaning me) really be mine?", question in his eyes. Nevertheless, the ropes were unfastened from the boat, their ends knotted together and left hanging over the edge of the pier, and we were off! Never again would I sit and listen to Jock's Danny or Meggie's Jock, dumb and awkward through lack of knowledge: tomorrow would be different! We cleared the harbour wall . . . and I promoted myself to FISHERMAN.

Mid-way across the bay the swell increased causing the small boat to spit and spray. "Pull on yer gear", I was ordered, "It's ower late fin yer

weet", to which words of wisdom I promptly responded. The G.P.O.
leggings came up to my thighs and fell back to my knees, but a leather
belt, also courtesty G.P.O., finally girded everything in an untidy
'burroch' round my slender midriff. Then the smock, which until now
had been a dirty yellow bundle, a one-up status symbol, carried carelessly
under my arm to create an air of superiority to my classmates, most of
whom were still at the 'fishing-off-the-rocks-with-a-cork' stage. This
article of protective clothing had lain around in its compacted state for
some considerable time, and now, as it creaked obstinately apart like an
old mizzen sail, my pride in the thing began to fade. But this was no time
to dwell on proverbs, or be distracted by their forebodings. A musty smell
rose from the newly unearthed creases, and when the huge waist was
finally prised open, the stench was overpowering. I shoved my head into
the gaping abyss and realised that the longer I dallied in its nauseous
tunnel the worse it would be. With a deep breath, and lungs full of
corrupt air, I thrust my head forward. Approximately three feet later, and
well off-course halfway down a sleeve, my head jammed fast in the elbow
section. 'Full Astern'! Panic-stricken and suffocating, I struggled to
remove the wide-mouthed yellow monster with its sick-smelling breath,
and finally managed, pulling myself back from the edge of unconscious-
ness. Looking aft, I noted the silent smirk on my father's face. Almost
willingly, I renewed my efforts, plunged into the vile depths a second
time, avoiding the 'MY God, is HE mine' eyes, and then SUCCESS—
I was through to fresh air at the top end. But the encounter had set in
motion a chain reaction with mumblings and rumblings inside the
yellow skin gathering momentum. Cold sweats, hot sweats, small
burps and large farts resulted, and the word 'seasick' registered in my
mind.

"Dae ye feel O.K.?", he asked, "Ye look awfa' fyte about the gills".

He was at least three colours out. I was green. The faint hope that he
was at last seeing me in a different light never entered my mind. Unsure
of my answer, I nodded diagonally.

The engine slowed and the lines were paid over the side. "Hang on", I
thought. "Start working, and you're cured". I held on. I held it down. But
the sight of the first string of mackerel flapping wildly over my boots,
the blood from their torn mouths, fresh, red and flowing freely, was the
final straw. The line slipped from my limp fingers, falling slack as it hit
bottom, then swished back and forth as the threshing fish tried to free
themselves. I dived for the rail. 'Huueghh', followed by some shorter
staccato 'heughs', and my corned beef sandwiches hit the sea. Fish
or no fish, work or want, I was ready for home and slid into the fish
'bree' in the bottom of the boat, more dead than alive. The cold
blood-streaked water ran inside my jacket and leggings, but nothing

could rouse me to an upright position. My father, determined to clear his mortgage the very first night, pulled in mackerel, string after string. The general fishing among the local fleet was slack that night except for the *Acorn* with seven hundredweights of prime mackerel. We never thought of it at the time, but we were the only boat using Libby's corned beef as a lure: my contribution to the evening's success. With perseverence, I eventually overcame my sickness, and the summer developed into one of extreme pleasure. The long sunny evenings flew past, and all too soon the mackerel season was over. But not without its rewards.

August meant lobsters. "Watch for the 'keeks' withering", we were advised, "that's seen enuff". With a lot of help from old Jock Danny—a retired fisherman—we had, over the summer months, acquired a grand total of fourteen creels ready to 'shoot'. They were stacked in ranks by our house, the 'beads' (ropes) coiled neatly on top, waiting for the braes to turn brown.

On a quite Saturday, with nothing better to do, a close friend and I slipped secretly away to the harbour. We carried a creel each, the beads over our shoulders. Determined not to be seen, we rowed *Acorn* to the rocks below Mhor, where we had already pre-planned to set the traps, hoping to surprise everyone with our ingenuity and a fresh lobster. For a long time we circled in search of a sandy hole to drop the first pot, but this became tedious, and at the first sight of yellow sand among the floating brown jungle of seaweed, I immediately threw a creel overboard. As it left my hands, I realised my mistake. I had not tied on the creel beads. Desperately I groped at the slowly sinking pot, and twice caught it by the 'eye' with an oar, only to see it slip off and sink another tempting foot. Already, through the season, we had lost hooks, flies and weights. But a CREEL was something else, coming only second to the boat in true worth. With no heart to shoot the second creel we decided to return to port, but not before cutting two fathoms of the three ply bead at different lengths to suggest a breakage. Despite this ill-fated start, the lobsters caught well in the remaining thirteen (lucky for some) creels, and equalled the mackerel fishing for profit. The early morning 'rising' and the late nights needed to haul them twice a day, became routine and was well rewarded. As for my little deceit, it was written in the annals of the 'not proven', for there was never an inquiry into the one per cent decrease in our fishing capacity.

On a muggy, drizzly night, at the back end of the season, we decided to give the mackerels one last try to satisfy ourselves that the shoals had left. The disagreeable weather meant we were the only boat to leave the harbour that night. We should have known better. Two miles east of the harbour our normally reliable engine 'hottered' to a standstill. Thinking this would be easily rectified, we continued to cast flies overboard. We drifted east in the strong swell and were soon out beyond the Head, only realising our position when a break in the clouds afforded an abrupt glance at the rocks, now far inside our position. After much heaving at the starter rope, and no sign of life, the oars were unleashed and I set to rowing, while father, wet and reeking of petrol, started dismantling the engine. Plugs, carburettor leads and filters lay higgledy piggledy on the stern seat. An oilskin sheet failed to keep them dry. In the midst of swearing and dripping sweat they were cleaned, replaced, and the string pulled. FAILURE! I heaved on the oars for two hours, slowly closing the distance to the harbour, while the lifeless engine was stripped down and rebuilt over and over again. With tempers fraying more at each vain attempt we finally reverted to manpower, and with an oar each we rowed for the harbour. Four hours after the engine had first faltered, and with aching arms, we arrived back at the pier. Before the engine was lifted into its storage bracket, I pulled the starter—'VROOM'—first time it burst into life. Caught completely by surprise, there was a stunned silence before we swore loud and long in unison.

With the previous night's adventure fresh in our minds, the engine was unbolted at low water and carried ashore. A bracket was furbished in the garden shed to which the machine was fastened and the sea-cock placed in a bucket of water. In these improved conditions the engine was again stripped and cleaned and immediately coughed into life. In the flush of success we opened the throttle and the whole thing sprang from the wall bracket and into gear, the wildly gyrating propeller coming within an inch of savagely amputating my father's left foot. Enough was enough— summer was over for both of us!

RONALD RITCHIE

Hopeman

The nets were brought home after a fishing, dried on the village green, and taken to the room in the house allotted for that purpose, where we girls learned from our mothers how to mend tears in them with a special needle and twine. I didn't mind the job at all although it was a bit monotonous, but being a big family, there were usually two or three of us taking part. I, being the youngest, dodged the big holes, leaving them to my older sisters. When the nets were mended they were stored away till the herring season began, when they had to be carried to the harbour. Two or even three horses and carts in the village vied with each other for the job of carting the nets, as one's work helped the other to make a living. The butcher, the baker and grocer never touched a herring net but all earned their daily bread from the same source—the sea.

GAVIN THOM

The Banishment

Da Philps stared at the shore from the stern of the small fishing boat, his black wool waistcoat and jacket dulling the sting of the bitter February breeze scudding over the sunlit waves. The children blethered excitedly at the novelty of being in the fish-scaled, tar-reeking yawl. In grim contrast, the adults' weatherbeaten faces held a fiery silence above the rummel of furniture and fidgeting bairns.

Usually easy pleased and easier led (or pushed) Da's fixed glower worried his wife, now hard and defiant in her victory. She watched him finger something shiny in his powerful hand, which he then let slip over the side and into the cold grey water. The 'plop!' was lost in the slap of the waves on the side of the small craft. Lizzie's eyes probed her husband's face but she couldn't decipher his thoughts as Da sullenly continued to watch the water. "Back far it should bide", he muttered. The object glinted as it fell, tumbling slowly through the water, out of the green light and into the green depths. He turned his grey head and his dark eyes absorbed the high black cliff and the old castle receding behind him, silhouetted against the luminous north horizon.

Da had never looked far into the future and now that it was crucial to do so, he seemed to be able to think only of the past. A man was well past his prime at forty-six; this was no time to start a new life. He took no part in the rowing, though his tall and muscular frame would have been of welcome assistance to his sons Davie, Dod, and Jimmy as they rowed the burdened craft through wave and wind. Thankfully the day was bright, although fresh and windy. It was a bitter contrast to the great gale only weeks before . . .

The old castle of Slains which now lay behind them had loomed over the Philps family for more than three hundred years. The houses themselves had been built on the scant and precarious stretch of flat land atop the massive sea cliffs and had been constructed from the grey and curiously metallic-sheened stones salvaged from the castle itself.

Between these rubble-built dwellings there was a proliferation of sheds, racks and upturned boats all smelling variously of fish, smoke and tar. Here fish would be cured, lines unravelled and carefully coiled, and hundred of hooks baited with mussels from earthenware jars.

Below this tiny plateau fell a visible testament to these hardy folk's persistence and diligence; a whole side of cliff composed of thousands upon thousands of shells discarded by the inhabitants over the centuries. It stretched from the top of the cliff down to the rocky shore a hundred and fifty feet below.

There, to the south, lay the small wooden boats, dragged above the high water mark out of reach of the fickle sea. Slightly above them, the shore path wound to the nearby village of Collieston, and alongside the path stood rows and rows of wooden racks where haddock would be hung to dry to become 'speldings'. Around and between these permanent fixtures ran a lively mixture of children, sheep, pigs and chickens.

In the summer Old Castle could have a silence so profound that it was undisturbed even by the ever-present gulls, the unearthly sound of their eerie, echoing, mewling cries seeming rather to expand the quiet. But like an evil enchantment the atmosphere of decay and of the past had a powerful inertia that gripped the area and infected the people within it. Things had not changed and would not change: Da Philps was part of that ancient, spellbound world.

In contrast, less than five miles away, the new 'Cruden Bay Hotel' had just been built. It's granite shone like a resplendent jewel among the green velvet of its golf courses, croquet lawns, tennis courts and bowling greens: it had been built for the wealthy who were now brought North by the new railway to Peterhead.

While the wet-legged and freezing fisherwomen of Slains carried their men on their backs from the boats, the electric tramway transported sun-hatted and lace-bedecked ladies from the railway station to the polished oak hall of the hotel. And while the fishers hauled the heavy-hulled boats on to the shingle, politicians and actors would wander from dining room or billiard room to one of the hotel's hundred bedrooms.

Da sat glowering in the salt-splashed yawl. That railways was always bringing more folk in: merchant bankers, factory owners, brewers, authors. The famous and wealthy seemed to be coming to take the air and sample the waters. The locals were doing well out of it—just a pity the railway hadn't come in past Collieston, then maybe there would be an easier market for the fish . . .

It must be fine for the folk in the big hotel to have taps though, and sinks, and even a bath right next to their beds. They didn't have to humph the water from the spring right to the top of the brae. And if you sent the bairns, the enamel pails were half empty by the time they stottered back up to the top! It was such a chav that the women would even carry the washing down to the rocks rather than take the water up. He looked at Lizzie as she tied her black knitted shawl tighter round her still auburn hair: she would work from before it was light to the guttering of the lamp—gathering mussels from the icy Ythan estuary—rousing the men and breaking their fast—organising the older bairns for school and then feeding and clothing the youngest. Lizzie's day was full with shelling and baiting; gutting and cleaning; salting and drying. Once the fish was prepared she would then have to carry a full basket upon her back, bound with a strap across her shoulders, to sell them in Peterhead twelve miles away, or barter them at the local farms for milk or oatmeal, cheese or tatties.

Da pictured the leaky roofed house with the millstone and the chair set on the flagstones in front. He remembered how the bairns, for their safety when very young, had been tied to the millstone lest they wander too far from their precarious home and perish by tumbling over the cliffs. He began to feel half as if he was just a bairn again himself. Perhaps in a way he was only now free of the millstone . . . and maybe this was how it felt to be falling through space . . .

Himself, his father, his father's father—all white-fishers. All had worked the lines close by the shore. The centuries reached back to the first Philps on this shore. Aye, that Philps had had a rougher time of it! . . . his Spanish galleon foundered, tossed by the uncaring waves onto barren rock; hundreds of his fellows drowned or battered to death on the shore; and himself washed up on a heretic land where no-one spoke his tongue. At least the Philps are leaving easier than they came, Da thought. But still not leaving easily . . .

"Da! Get a hud o Teeny. She's hauf o'er the side!"

Da jolted out of his reverie, grabbed the quine and lifted her up by her middle. She had been staring, fascinated, into the deep grey water. He sighed resignedly as he noticed Teeny's feet; one in a shoe and one in a boot . . .

But even Da could not ignore the significance of the latest storm, nor forget its fierceness. Many times in the past the gales had been so wild that the panes of glass in the tiny cottage windows had been cracked by shells blown right up from the shore far below. But this storm was far worse than any other in living memory. Twenty miles away the telegraph lines had been blown down, and even in Aberdeen the town clocks had been stopped dead by the ferocity of the blizzard.

Always a windy area, Buchan grows few trees even yet, and Old Castle lay in a very exposed location, open on three sides to the sea and the driving wind. Expecting poor weather at this time of year, the men had kept a close eye on the sky and had noticed an unusual darkening of the horizon until the edge of the sky was a foreboding brownish hue. Fearing extreme conditions ahead, the men dragged the boats further up the rocky and grassy slope until they were a good thirty feet above high sea level. Everything about the place was made fast and the villagers prepared for what they expected would be just another of the many storms which regularly strafed that coast.

But as the storm grew nearer, an early darkness came with it, the wind escalated and despite their preparations, baskets and wooden tubs began to be blown about the village. The darkness seemed to amplify their sense of hearing: the roof tiles rattled, the ropes and riggings whistled, the chimneys howled and the doors and windows creaked and shook as if they would be riven by the squally gusts.

Outside the foam and froth spewed upwards, mixing with sleet and cloud in an unholy freezing drench of sea and sky. As tiles peeled off to smash unheard in the din, wooden sheds tumbled to fly through space. The waves roared and flew into the lum caves nearby, causing fountains of spume to explode into the sky, crashing and howling in the shriek of the wind.

Water bowies thick with ice rocked and tumbled, spilling their contents on the spray-soaked, slush-laden flagstones outside the poor dwellings. Children screamed in terror while grown men had to hide their fear. They prayed to their God while they pulled on ganzies and oilskins to salvage what they could.

Inside the besieged cottages snow and sleet built up round the forgotten gaps and chinks in the crumbling masonry, and whipped through every crack in the old wooden doors. The dim orange glow of lamps glittered off green glass floats swinging dreamily from the rafters, the faint soft light reflecting from pottery mugs and the tear-streaked faces of small children. Mothers stoked up the low fires to brightness despite the damp, while the smoke curled treacherously back down the sodden stone chimneys. All night the storm raged and rumbled . . .

The next day light did not come. Still the cloud, mist and sleet stayed on to add misery to destruction. A dreary greyness came upon the village, like dull light off a dogfish's back, but enough to see the boats that lay smashed, scattered about the shore in crazy disarray. Seaweed and filthy sand-sodden suds lapped the rocks and paths; lines ripped, frayed, and tangled had been hunted out from their places of safe-keeping and flung like black garlands upon the rocks, grass and walls; and terrified sheep, forgotten in the tempest, had been thrown from their cropped and softsmooth grazing to the limb-wracking boulders below. Where once there had been racks for speldings, now only the stunted and snapped bases of the poles remained: the frames of the racks were never to be seen again.

More frightening yet were the everyday objects which whispered horribly of barely-imagined terrors elsewhere: oars and spars, a tall leather sea-boot and cork life-perservers tossed fifty foot up on the shore. The damage to the houses too was telling . . . Lizzie looked more than usually concerned as the men began to repair boats, patch roofs, mend lines. Her brown brow knotted as she watched, not for the first time, the village begin to heal itself once more from its winter wounds.

About a fortnight later, as young Davie was guiding the yawl to the shore, Da was surprised to see so many folk upon the shore. He had expected Lizzie standing ready to carry him out of the boat to keep his sea-boots dry, but with her he spied the children, all lined up and capering excitedly. As the yawl swelled nearer he began to make out what the bundles beside them were. Bedding lay trussed and packaged; their poor sticks of moveable furniture were stacked alongside; and he recognised everyday stuff from about the house lying scattered ominously on the multi-coloured pebbles of the shore: pots, jars, ropes, buckets and pans. A few wooden kists, presumably full of the smaller stuff, lay beside them. Lizzie's face held an expression of resigned determination. Da's stomach sank at the sight. Davie behind him, head hung, muttered: "I hid meant ti tell ye Da . . ."

As the keel of the boat scraped shingle and the boys steadied with the oars, Lizzie, arms folded, shouted towards them:

"There's nae future here for my children. We're leaving . . . Now."

And so Da came to be fingering the shiny Spanish dollar. His stomach still felt queer. It felt worse when he realised he would have nowhere to lie down to ease it. His family might well be the sons of that captain of cavalry, come with the Spanish Armada, he thought, but that was a good long while ago. He sniffed the salt air as he saw they were approaching Collieston.

Saint Catherine's Dub lay before him, where the galleon *Santa Caterina* had been smashed, along with the hopes of Spain, three hundred years before. It was here the Philps' seed had been planted on the Scottish shores. Not knowing what he was doing, on impulse, he let the dollar slip into the sea, to join the rest of the past six fathoms below.

"Back far it should bide," he muttered . . .

But as he let the loss flow over him, there warmed an unexpected inward spark of hope. The face of his cousin's daughter came into his mind's eye; black-haired, dark-eyed and olive skinned; Sarah, every inch a Spaniard—already folk called her 'Black' Sarah. Da laughed. His wife and children had hardly noticed. Just as well, he didn't know why he had laughed himself.

As the short winter's day drew on, they covered the twenty miles to Aberdeen and the small sail was lowered as they passed the pier and came in sight of the old roundhouse. The huge harbour with its cranes, bridges, and giant-masted sailing ships dwarfed the old yawl as it was rowed painfully towards Torry and the southern shore.

"Davie!" "Lizzie!" Shouts rang from the shore. Da's brother Jimmy waved them towards him.

"Weel done, weel done. C'mon in by!" Jimmy indicated an easy berth alongside. Beside him stood his daughter, laughing at the confusion.

"Hello Betty, Maggie! Dod, Jock and Tam are all here to meet ye!" Da could make out more of his own folk in the rowdy crowd; cousin Robert, his brothers; his weary eyes picked out the faces. The families from the village too, old Sandy Milne in duffle jacket and black peaked cap among them. Da had never thought to see so many there.

"Ye've made it hiv ye?" grinned old Sandy.

Da watched befuddled as his many children, one by one, took their first steps in Torry. He realised that those steps would lead each to his or her own destiny; whether in prosperity, in disgrace, or in doom.

His thoughts were interrupted as old Sandy gripped him by the arm his clear old eyes reading Da's confused emotions;

"Aye," he said quietly, nodding towards the crowd, "it disna look like banishment when an auld man sees aboot him his family an his freens."

Note: Da Philps, though forty-six when he 'migrated', enjoyed another forty years in his adopted home. His many children, spurred on by the unceasing concern and unflagging energy of their mother Lizzie, did very well in the city.

The Philps were just a few of the sixtý-six people who abandoned the ancient fishing village of Old Castle, Slains, in March 1900. They, like many, many others from small towns and villages throughout the North East, left all that they knew, and held dear, to seek a new life in the rising fishing industry of Torry. It was the efforts of these people, and many others like them, that led the city of Aberdeen to grow, to thrive, and to prosper.

GREGOR J R PHILLIPS

Winter '77

Cold,
manifesting itself
in ice
on the inside of windows,
a quarter inch thick.

Dawn,
the brightness of angels,
flooding my room
and startling the world,
with all-piercing light.

Frost;
numb hands, icy breath,
clearing windscreen and lock.
Joining traffic
on roads brown with sand.

Queue.
A cobblestone side-road;
boxes, lorries,
men in bright aprons
and wives with red hands.

Fish
is their livelihood,
fish fill the boxes,
fish fills the air;
Whilst the Dee sleeps, frozen.

JOAN McKICHAN

Rich Man, Poor Man

The lairds of Brodie, Cumming and Kintessack sat playing cards with the laird of Culbin one Saturday night. The firelight crackled peaceably in the stone hearth but as the evening wore on a storm began to brew outside, battering against the casement and rattling the slates on the roof.

"Weel, Culbin, it's gettin' gie late." Brodie pushed back his chair. "It's time I was awa'."

"Surely no? The nicht's young yet."

"No' that young. An' jist listen tae the wind blawin' up."

Cumming added, "I've a good ten mile tae ride roon' the Bay. I'll need awa' afore the wind turns east intae ma face."

"Weel, weel, then. Maybe *you* maun go. But the ithers can bide a whilie yet, can ye no?"

"Whit!" grumbled Kintessack. "An' let ye rook me o' a' ma siller? Na, na, I'm awa' hame while I still hae a twa three pennies in ma pooch!"

Brodie chipped in, irritated beneath his cheerfulness, "Me an' a'. Ye'd think a man we' a' your tack wid let his freends win a haun' o' cairds noo and then, but nivver a bit o'it!"

Culbin laughed. "Fit maks ye think I'm rich? Dae ye no ken, the tax man takes mair aff me nor aff ony ither boddy in the hale o' Scotland."

"Aye, aye," Kintessack said, "so ye're aye saying'. But ye've still mair in yer kist than the lave o' us pit thegither, eh?"

'Wi' your acres ye canna lose, can ye?" commented Cumming. Spitefully he added, "Yer 'land that cam' as a lean fae God'. Ye ken fit they say!"

Culbin tossed his head crossly. "I'm nae wolf! It was bocht fair an' square at the Dissolution! It's no ma fault it wis aince Abbey land."

"An' fair's fair, Cumming," Brodie pointed out. "That wis near two hunner' 'eer sine. It's a gie lang string ye're tying tae the chiel!"

"It wis still kirk land," insisted Cumming.

"The Auld Kirk though. And King's land afore that," Brodie mused. "Ye could say it should ha' gaed back intae royal haun's aifter."

"Weel, it has!" snapped Culbin, annoyed at the ill will of his friends. "Far dae ye think a' thae taxes end up? I'm nae mair nor the labourer—an' I seem tae be the puir feel payin' the hire an' a'!"

"Ye dinna look puir tae me," Kintessack said frankly, eyeing the fine silk on Culbin's back. He picked up a brocaded vest slung carelessly over the back of a tapestry chair. "Foo muckle for this tawdry tatter? Worth a bet or twa?"

"Or three," conceded Culbin, simmering down. "Man, but ye're a girny lot the nicht, a' ower a puckle lost pennies!—It's yer ain skill ye shid hae a look at."

"Skill? Ca' yon skill!" Kintessack snorted. "An' if it's skill ye're aifter ye maun hae anither look for hairvesters in bye. D'ye ken fit thae itinerants are up tae noo? Aifter a' the trouble we hid last year?"

"Ye hinna taen in the traivellers fae Perth again, hiv ye?" Brodie complained angrily. "Ye ken fine fit they got up tae afore. Hiv ye tellt them tae leave the girse alain this time?"

"Fit girse?" asked Cumming, noting the dismay in the faces of Brodie and Kintessack.

"Thon marram," Culbin explained. "The stuff grouwin' ower the dunes.—I canna dae that. They need it tae thatch their biggin'."

"Oh, aye?" Brodie scolded. "If ye didnna gie them a richt billet they'll bigg their ain fast eneuch. Fa wints tae sleep in the hairst fields?"

Culbin defended himself, "If I gie them a billet I hae tae pay that masel', an' that comes aff fit I gie them. They'll no come for fit's left."

"It disna hiv tae come aff their pay," objected Brodie. "Yer pooch is deep eneuch tae cover that, surely. If they're that good at the work?"

"Na, na. If I did that, it wid be as cheap gittin' in the locals."

Brodie and Kintessack exchanged despairing looks. "It's fit we dae."

"An' nane left for me," Culbin triumphed. "Ye've swicket me oot o' them! Na, I'll haud on like I aye did. An' ma faither afore me."

"This girse?" asked Cumming again. "This marram? It's no the stuff that binds the sand wi' its roots, is't? Ye're at a gie shauky game if ye let them howk that up—I mine ma faither sayin' . . ."

"Ach, yer faither's auld eneuch to be deed noo, ma mannie," laughed Culbin, anxious to end the conversation. "Are ye goin'? Because if ye're nae, we could hae anither haun'."

"Goin'," Cumming said bluntly, pulling on his great coat. At the door he turned back and shook his finger at his host. "But thae auld monks at Kinloss had a thocht or twa in their nappers, for a' their Popish ways. They widna let that girse be touched. Swore the sand wid walk if it wis."

"Aye," Kintessack returned gloomily to the argument. "An' walkin' is jist wit it's daein'. A' ower my best acres jist tae the west o' Findhorn Bay."

"And mine," Brodie added, "in ahin the bar on the beach. So that's ane on eether side o' yer 'granary o' Scotland'. I'm warnin' ye. Ye'll live tae pay mair in the end than ye've saved wi' yer traivellin' scythers. Wheat disna grouw in sand. Ye'd better keep yer e'en on them."

A loud knocking made them all turn towards the door.

"Fegs," muttered Culbin. "It's a queer time for visitin'!"

"It is that," said Cumming. "But ye can open the door and let me oot while ye spier at fa wints in."

The three visiting lairds left, pushing against a ferocious gale past a tall, handsome man clad in a heavy, black coat and top hat.

"Come in, come in, mannie, till I sneck the door. Ye've picked a rouch nicht for callin'!"

"I seem to have lost my way." The stranger spoke in very polished English tones.

"Well, ye'd better bide the nicht.—Dae ye play a haun' o' cairds maybe? There's still an hour till the Sabbath comes in."

"I do indeed. But my stakes are high."

"Dinna fash yersel'. I've got plenty tae bet wi'."

The two men sat down to play, the stranger keeping his black top hat on his head in spite of invitations to remove it. The laird of Culbin's winning streak continued but the stranger seemed well able to pay his losses and handed over his cash with a good grace. Suddenly the splendid Dundee clock struck midnight, twelve silvery chimes. Culbin prepared to pack up but the stranger looked up in surprise.

"Man, dae ye nae ken we're intae the Sabbath noo?" Culbin asked cheerfully. "I doobt ye've been lost langer than ye thocht!"

The stranger smiled slightly. "So it seems. But the Sabbath has as many hours and minutes as any other day. Why should we think of it as different?

"But it's the Lord's Day. Ye canna play cairds on the Lord's Day!" He looked at the stranger closely, not all together liking the faint look of contempt.

"There is a certain lack of logic in that, surely? If it is the Lord's Day, will He not protect what you do on that day?—Or are you afraid that your luck is about to run out?"

Stung, Culbin snapped, "It's nae luck that gar's me win! It's skill!"

"Yet you are unwilling to prove it?" was the silky reply. Deliberately the stranger laid down another card, while his eyes measured with those of Culbin. Culbin was puzzled by this behaviour, even a little afraid. For long minutes the Dundee clock chattered on and the stranger's smile deepened scornfully. Finally Culbin laid a card of his own.

On through the night the two played in silence. One struck, then two and Culbin became gloomier with each game. By three the laird was worried, while the stranger remained totally unperturbed.

"Weel, I think it's time for bed, eh?" Culbin stood up at last.

"You're not quitting when your luck is down, are you?"

"Och, it's jist that it's gettin' a wheen late."

"Just one more game might turn the tide."

Culbin looked awkward. "Hm. Weel, tae be honest—I doobt I hinna ony mair siller in the hoose. I maun stop. I'm nae a cheat, whitever they say."

"I'll take a promise. You're sure to win it back in any case."

Culbin shook his head doubtfully. "Fit wid ye tak? I hinna a thing that wid be ony eese tae the likes o' you."

The stranger thought for a few moments. "Mm?—What about—Ayh, I've got it. What about staking one acre of your land for all the money on this table? That's the entire winnings of the evening."

Culbin thought to himself, "That's ower good a bet tae pass." But he was worried. Yet . . . "Richt! Ye're on! Play a caird."

They played and Culbin began to look gloomy. Eventually he lost the hand. "Ye've got yerself an acre, my freen'. Just as well I've a wheen mair far that cam' fae."

"Enough to stake the same bargain again? One acre against all my winnings?"

"Oh, aye," Culbin cheered up. "That's worth anither try or twa." But another acre was lost, and yet one more. Still the stranger offered the same bargain, and still the laird hoped for one lucky hand which would win back all his losses. Outside the storm raged fiercely. With the wind blowing out of the north, the sea crashed over the grass free dunes. The sands came rolling southwards, swallowing up the good land and turning it into desert, acre by acre, while the men played on till dawn.

By then Culbin was frantic. "Man, man, ye nivver lose, dae ye? Nae a single haun' since midnicht!"

"I did warn you that my stakes were high."

In a fury Culbin raged, "Ye've been waur nor the tax man wi' yer lum hat aye on yer heed. For pity's sake tak it aff and gang tae yer bed!"

"For pity's sake?" With a grim smile he took it off, revealing two small, neat horns on his head. He waved the hat towards the window where a queer, yellow dawn was appearing, the light struggling through sand which had silted almost to the top of the casement. Culbin stared in horror, first at the horns and then at the sand.

"Oh, preserve me! Oh, Heaven protect me!—Whaur's a' thon come fae?"

Not in the least surprised the stranger spoke. "Out of the north. But will you not play on? Same bargain as before? I took your promise. Will you not take mine now?"

In utter despair Culbin gazed at his visitor. "Wi' a' thon sand blawin' up tae the rooftops I doobt I hinna ony option."

Some say that they are still playing cards to this day, deep beneath the Sands of Culbin. Now and then a twisted crab apple tree would appear, or a spindly bush in the desert would produce a sad little rosebud, all that was left of the rich land below. Men came and planted trees, but the sand crept in once more and swallowed them up. More men came with more trees, but this time they began by replanting the old marram grass. Now there are pine forests, and glades with sandy bottoms, and the ospreys have returned to hunt in the great bay of Findhorn. The abbey of Kinloss is now no more than a rickle of ruins within a lonely churchyard. But the wisdom of the monks lives on.

MARGARET WOODWARD

Nae Fit It Wis

There's nae mair shally roadies
An' nae mair speldin' racks
An' ye'll nae see booed aul craiters
Muckle creels upon their backs
Nae weemin sheilin' mussels

An' naeb'dy reddin' lines
There's nae mair dances in the hall
Tho' we've aye some bonnie quines
Ye'll nae see aul' Tam Walker
Wi' his wither-beaten smile
An'ither couthy characters
Hiv wear't awa as fyle
Cotie, Buckie, Jocky Mey:
Toonie Sot an' Tammie Boo;
Aul' Toolie an' Jimmicky-
Tae name but just a few
But a' them and the likes o' them
Have gaen an' left a miss
An' Collieston's jist nae the same
But let me tell ye this—
Fyles I hear the clunk o'oars
Fan there's nae a yoal in sicht
An' the clump o'leather sea-beets
On an impty pier at nicht
Fyles a burst o' laachin'
Comes fae ben alang the shore
That I'd sweir wis Sarah Helen
Like she ees't tae laach afore
An' its nae imagination
Thro' an alcoholic fog
For it's nae on Hogmanay I've seen
Kye grazin' in the bog.
I've heard a spunk bein' crackit
On the gunnel o' a yoal
An' turn't an' lookit roun' aboot
An' nivver seen a soul
Bit—fits mair oot the ord'nar'
Wiz yon whiff o' Bogie Roll.
Ye'll maybe nae believe me
An' I'll let ye hae yer say
But, *I ken* there's naeb'dy hereaboot
Smokes Bogie Roll the day.

                              JOHN ROBERTSON

THE LAND

Axes

I have always found wood fires attractive. You can look into them as they collapse into heaps of little glowing dice. I've never been much into seeing pictures in the fire, as people were apparently wont to do ages ago, but I do like the little dice and the heat and, of course, the smell—sharp and spicy, changing as the wood burns away, and differing from wood to wood, from the rounded scent of ash to the acrid resin of pine. The thought of cheap heat and a powerful hint of hedonism was what led me to join three neighbours in a wood-cutting venture one summer, deluded no doubt by dim memories of lumberjacking derring-do from school geography lessons.

All done of course with a proper contract from the Forestry Commission. 'To be cleared by such and such a date . . . appropriate safety equipment . . . rollover bars on timber tractors', plus many other obscure and mandatory hints.

A survey of the site made us think a bit. Three acres or so of 'firewood quality' spruce. This meant that in the interests of cost-cutting the trees had never been thinned. Mirroring the economic philosophy behind the cost-cutting, the weaklings struggled for light and those that had made it reared their heads above the others, their trunks oozing gobs of triumphant resin. It was not possible to push through the trees, and the heart of our little forest was impenetrably dark and probably troll-ridden. To complicate matters, the winter's storms had whittled away at the periphery of the area, snapping trunks a few feet from the ground or causing whole trees to lounge affectionately against their neighbours. Further to this, the whole lot resided on a slope looking west, and the forestry road ran round the base of the slope. So all this had to be cut and carried to the roadside! Suddenly even the runts looked daunting.

The first evening I went out was a wet summer's evening. Not pouring, but just a steady soggy drip, deceptively wet and penetrating. Leaden sky, no wind, on the cold side of mild, an average summer evening for Buchan. Since I had no chainsaw, I'd sharpened up my felling axe hitherto used for kindling and we set off in the old Peugeot, playing at 'Special Stages' on the forest roads. One of the great things about being an adult is that you never really grow up. All the trappings change though, which is one of the saddest parts.

I'd spent a while sharpening the axe, which had hacked through innumerable nails in odd boxes and pallets, musing the while that the scrape of sharpening stones must have been around since axes began.

My mate started the yellow and black chainsaw, and with a howl like a giant wasp a mouth of startling paleness appeared at the base of the first tree amid a whirl of chips and shavings. Then round to the back of the mouth, a despairing creak and down it went. I'd elected to sned the trees, so I pushed in among the spiky feathers to the scaly trunk and stripped off the branches close to the main stem, working up one side and down the other. The tree's symmetry lay wrecked around it in subtly different shades of needled green. Then we cut the tree into carriable logs and I trimmed any remaining branches before stacking them.

As my muscles eased and warmed the unaccustomed labour became easier. The axe zipped straight through most branches with a most satisfying 'clunk'. The light began to fade and I was struggling knee deep in a dozen trees' worth of wet pine fronds. Axe-swinging was a little wild, and odd twinges on my palms proved of course to be resin-sticky blisters. As I dried off in the pub where wet boiler suits are quite acceptable wear, I felt a grim satisfaction. A few pints ended the first evening, though my shoulders ached for a day or two.

A deeply rutted track and firebreak combined marked the eastern border of our piece of forestry, and at the top of the track was, is, and I expect shall be, a collection of big boulders, a small ring with some others in the centre, hunched in the long grass of a little glade, hedged around with the artifice of modern forestry. It's a prehistoric tomb of no great merit, which rates a mention in local guide books and sundry antiquarian monographs. Not really much to look at, I thought a few days later, laying my axe against one of the old grey rocks. Looking down the track from my seat on one of the outer stones, there still seemed an awful lot of trees to go. We passed around our sandwiches and drank orange squash prior to wrecking the silence again. A few crumbs had ended up on the flat stone in the middle, and I flicked them off. It was somebody's tomb after all. The racket of chainsaws was insult enough.

With four of us in the group, and three chainsaws, my axe was still in use as work progressed. The piles of logs grew, and here and there, like sunlight through old curtains, odd glints of light showed that the trees were giving ground. My role in the assault was to clear the first few feet of each tree. This made access easier for the chainsaw wielders, since, firstly, the little dry branches sometimes snagged in the chain, and second, and certainly more importantly, using a chainsaw at face height whilst crouching around tree trunks is not a good idea. The simple axe can be used safely at close quarters; it will not asphyxiate with blue smoke nor will it bereave or maim, and it will always start first go.

The axe and my hands had matured quite quickly. Convenient thick skin grew on the high wear areas, and the pale ash shaft of the axe darkened with resin providing a non-slip surface.

We had been able, as time went by, to see how the professional slick salesmen went about their business using a tractor to help. We were lucky enough to arrange a loan of one, plus a long chain.

This creature was a venerable Fordson Major, very weatherbeaten and minus lights, silencer and so on, as are most tractors of that era. On the plus side, it started first time and every time and was forest-legal in that it had a roll bar. It also had the novel feature of chains on the rear wheels, large versions of the small snow chains for cars, which provided a troika-like overtone to the bass exhaust and mezzo-soprano transmission whine when running full tilt on the forestry road. Driving this antique over the hillside was quite a new experience. Any faster than dead slow was impossible, but what was impressive was its seemingly inexorable progress. The rear wheels would slip momentarily before the chains bit and it would ponderously claw over the treestumps, the blind blue nose shuffling the deepening piles of brushwood aside. You had to watch the treestumps though, even though they were cut short. Like a sailor aware of hidden reefs, I'd chart a course avoiding high stumps to reach the worksite. Despite the generous ground clearance, it could run aground, the sump jammed dead centre so that neither rear wheel could grip, but merely hurled showers of mushroom smelling needles around from the now exposed forest floor.

And what precisely did the tractor do, apart from crawling around? The long chain with an ominous nut and bolt holding two links together, had a big hook at the free end, the other being on the drawbar. We passed the hook and chain under a cut and shedded trunk and slipped the links into the hook forming a loop. When the tractor took up the slack, the loop tightened so you could tow the trunk. So it was; cut, sned, line up half a dozen trunks, poke the chain under all six and then drag the bunch over the hillside to the forestry road. Then they could be zipped into sections ready for trailers or lorries or whatever else we had borrowed.

The laden journey across the hillside made the tractor think a bit. Coal black smoke and the odd flash of yellow flame bore testimony to a weary engine. The Fordson was no longer a farmer's pride and joy in shiny blue and orange: the distinctive badge on the nose was gone too. Few people realise what a neat little piece of art deco design it was: the hand clasping the barley, surrounded by a stylised gear wheel, all straight from a five year plan poster. The tractor wasn't much interested either, never missing a beat as it lugged the naked trunks over the clearing hillside. The chain links tore into the bark, which oozed pungent, sticky sap. The innocent wood wasps' homes were cut, stripped, dragged and wrecked.

The biggest tree in the plot had abandoned itself to its fate even before we arrived, leaning resignedly on its neighbours at a forty-five degree angle. We cleared a glade around the trunk, which was a daunting three feet thick at the base. You could almost stand in the hole under the roots. Even leaned over, the crest still reared proud and bushy over the other trees, sharp against the sky. Just as woodcutters must have always done, we stood around talking and making grandiloquent gestures, many on the 'bell-the-cat' theme. Who in their sane senses would climb half way up with a chainsaw in a daring emulation of a Tom and Jerry sequence? Since we were sensible grownups we cut through the base. This required some fine judgement, since the trees could not fall normally. Cutting too far across the diameter one way would allow the cut to close under pressure and thus lock the chainsaw into the trunk. Some tricky slot-cutting in the upward facing part, and some anxious shoulder-wrenching cuts underneath holding a chainsaw at near arm's length, kneeling down and exerting upward pressure, all in poor visibility because of the fumes and woodchips, concentrating hard, yet with fearful thought of accidents caused the trunk to drop about half an inch, jammed against its base. You could hardly tell it was cut through. But the last twitch of this guillotined aristocrat would not avail. The tumbril arrived and the chains went on. A generous helping of hard throttle drummed out, eclipsing the resin with deisel as I took up the slack and let the clutch in with a thump, whipping the trunk off its cut stump. Our leviathan lay helpless, and just like a well-trained flensing crew, we moved in.

I had to tow the trunk blunt end first. Having got underway, I was standing at the wheel like an anxious pilot when there was a jerk and a vision of the tractor's scarred bonnet rising above me. Somehow I stomped on the clutch and grabbed the hand throttle and an even keel was resumed with a mighty crash. The great log end dug in and found a stump of an earlier planting, so the faithful tractor's fruitless exertion meant that it tried to scramble over backwards. I wasn't keen to test the roll bar and I cringed mentally, remembering the nut and bolt holding the chain together. Would the chain have flicked by my head, causing a fright, but a good story in the pub, or would it have been some ghastly tit-for-tat? No harm done, and we all laughed anyway.

One evening in early autumn, with an extension on our contract safely negotiated, everything went beautifully. The day was like summer, one of those nostalgic heartbreakers which hint of mortality, another year on its way out. We came back in the evening and the chainsaw and bass tractor harmonised in some sort of industrial unity. The appalling racket seemed to fit with the baring hillside's shoulder where contours now were almost clear. The last tree was silhouetted stark against the darkening eastern sky, only to fall amid a two-stroke howl. Its fronds were ripped off as the shadows crept up the track. The tomb's old grey stones took on an amaranthine glow as the light reached them once more. Time to go home though and we gathered our gear.

Not quite all of it though. My old axe was nowhere. Not in the car boot amid saws, gloves, leggings, ear protectors and other accoutrements. I hadn't been using it either, and I felt a sudden pang. I knew we would not find it, no matter how we looked. Amid the now countless fronds and soft piled needles it had gone for ever. No more would I sharpen the scarred blue painted head and feel the sureness of the weight.

The final stage of the wood clearing was to haul the remaining logs off the hillside. Since those earlier victims were in short sections the drag chain was hopeless. Borrowing a farm bogie to load them on to was easy enough, but hauling it on a steep hillside amid treestumps was hazardous. Some old stumps from a previous planting were higher than ours. A slight misjudgement, a rolled trailer, broken towing pin and much labour were caused. The perpetrators had to go. As I'd already demonstrated, the old Fordson's pull was impressive, so we scrabbled away some dirt around the first old stump, linked up the chain. The rear wheels ripped away branches and the thin topsoil. Well dug in, the bright chains gripped and the stump rolled over. The next one was bigger. Twice the chain slipped off before it bit into the decayed wood. The tractor exhaust plumed black and the front axle drummed and clashed as I popped the clutch in and out. Brutal treatment, but tremors and tiny rivulets of red dirt showed some promise before the inevitable rip and crunch. A pebble strewn hole about three feet deep was left. And an axe! I'd seen such things in museums, with dreary little labels beside them, but never found one. A real stone axe, passed again from hand to hand and 'Aren't you lucky! Lose one, win one!'

I took it home and gave it a good scrub with nailbrush and modern detergent. The dirt gone, revealed the marks on the stone, the tiny glitters of mica against the greenish grey grit. Somebody with a lot of patience had spent a lot of time on that, I thought. They're not easy to do, stone axes. There are heaps of rejects in the Lake District, bearing mute testimony no doubt to torn fingernails and curses in an old, old language. Whoever it was had done well with my axe though. I squinted at its symmetry and tossed its balance from hand to hand. A lot of skill and patience fairly flowed from it as I held it and turned it around.

A few weekends later, we finished on the hillside. The logs were all sorted off in safety and the branches shed their needles like acres of Christmas past. Bonfire Night came round, and to boost the flames of winter defying ritual we went back on the hill for a trailer load of brushwood, retracing the old course now not so familiar. It was silent, no saws, no occasional tourists' curious glances at native workmen. The old grey stones of the tomb were damp and nearly black now with the November chill. No mica sparkle, and the lichen on their surface was not an elusive pastel shade at all, but slimy grey.

Another old year's dying lay over the loom of the dark hillside. The poorly lit sky obscured the neat field lines and the harsh concrete sheds. I realised suddenly why the tomb was there. With the trees gone, you see clear away to the west and see the sun's dive from its midsummer's zenith to its low-level nadir.

That evening, I remembered a visit made years ago to some gloomy mansion, a mausoleum of monumental furniture, all the worst of Victorian tastelessness. In their restless materialism, they would leave nothing alone and undecorated or 'improved' in the crazy belief that progress would lead somewhere.

Someone in the family had dug open a couple of barrows nearby, and the spoils reposed in small glass cases. Flint arrow heads, a few potsherds and most poignant and distasteful, some surprisingly white teeth and bone fragments in a box. Surely the people had not taken all the trouble to shift all the earth from the grave so that some improvement busybody a mere three thousand years later would dig it all up again? The unchanging swirls of stars and planets that they knew gave eternity some meaning that the Victorians did not know. Given food and hunting game, the old men could stride through eternity, finding their way with ease.

On the shortest day, I slipped out of the house and cycled up to the woods. I headed for the chambered cairn of course. I took the axe from my pocket, and crouched to part the damp brown grass around the central stone before pushing the axehead a good arm's length under the central slab.

Straightening up, the roll and curve of the hillside took on a gentle glow from the pale sun, far over and resting on the western horizon. For a moment, everything felt right. Future and past and next payday meant nothing. Just a moment's exultation flashed at being part of a continuation of the silence, and not the self centre of a dizzy maelstrom, headlong willy-nilly for middle age and death.

The old people have their axe back, and I'm back at the vortex again, but at least I had my moment.

CHRISTOPHER BUTCHER

Bothy Folk

A farm bothy of the late 1930s or early 1940s: the last room of a row of stock housing—the one with the chimney! A spartan interior spiced with an assortment of odours from clothes and boots whose smells identified the class of stock their owners worked with—stale milk, horse sweat, cow dung and human feet. And a typical farm bothy dweller of the same period: single, upwards of middle age, a long serving employee who sleeps in his long drawers. The last description would neatly exclude myself and the friends who shared a bothy with me around that time. We were young, recently arrived, and we slept in a shirt, short drawers or nothing at all, depending on the season. The bothy was really a comfortless extension of the stables, where we slept between coarse blankets. The floor was uncovered concrete and there was no toilet. The preferred method was to take a spade and find a convenient hedge—a sort of mechanised version of the method used by cats.

My employer used to leave my wages, on a Saturday morning, in the toe of my boot at the foot of my stair. This was usually some change wrapped in a note, and not very bulky. Once I decided to drop a hint, and pretended to have worn my boot all day without noticing the money.

There was a sort of heirarchy among the farm workers of that period. Being a horseman (ploughman) conferred more status than being a cowman. Shepherds—particularly of the hill variety—stood alone, a race apart, separated by their specialisation and solitary life style. Pig men? Well, you just didn't talk about it. Many of us milked cows and worked horses between milking, but we tended to lay conversational emphasis on the horse work.

I suppose the passage of time lends enchantment to memories. I can still close my eyes and imagine the scrape of soil off a plough 'wreast' and smell the sweat drifting back from a fine pair of Clydesdales. I can forget about lacing up hard leather boots with hands painfully chapped with the cold, and the endless days walking behind harrows. Perhaps I might be forgiven if I romanticise a time, when, footloose and fancy free, with all I owned in the world in one old suitcase, I was free come term day—28th May or 28th November—to decide my fate for the next six months. This was the time to negotiate a new contract or go in search of fresh pastures. During those early years as an intinerant farm worker, I developed a great interest in the work and a love of the land, that is with me still. My life has been spent nudging mother nature to produce a little more, to turn sand into gold, but always with the knowledge that we had to work in harmony. If I draw a give and take line through life's good times and bad I find a thread which runs through, constant and faithful like a good marriage: a love affair with the land which started so long ago.

Who said it wouldn't last!

IAN C THOMSON

Women's Work

Although she was a good few years past her three score and ten, grandma rose about five every morning and worked on the farm till seven in the evening—fussing about with her clokkin' hens, tending young turkey chicks (which she maintained were "afa' delicate"), filling up huge iron pots with tatties and turnips, which, after cooking over the open peat fire, were mixed with mash to feed the laying hens and also the 'swine'. (Never did I hear her say 'pigs'!)

Grandma had been widowed twenty years back and had bravely soldiered on ever since—feeding her calves at the park gate with warmed milk poured into wooden cogs or with the many more chores to do with the livestock on the sixty-six acre farm that had been worked by her father and grandfather before her. She slept in the wee bedroom off the kitchen, it being the warmest in the house, and, of course, grandma had a feather bed—not like mine, which was filled with chaff! On the day the threshing mill came the tykes were filled from the heap of chaff that had gathered at the end of the mill. The job had to be done that day in case it rained before morning. The bed was so full up that first night it almost touched the ceiling, with me usually ending up landing on the floor. After a night or two things settled down however, and by the time the threshing mill came a year on, the chaff was almost turned to dust.

I glanced up through the skylight to a clear blue sky. A shaft of warm sunshine fell across my cheek—another day's forkin' at the hairst I thought . . . I got dressed quickly and clumped down the stairs, heavy of foot, from the thick leather shoes grandma insisted I wear. These shoes had originally been boots sent to the soutar to have the ankles cut off. But not enough! The edges dug into the knobbly bits on my ankles. The heels had metal rings attached, and the soles were covered in rows of tackets! I tied the strings of my long grey apron round my slender waist and traipsed through to the milk cellar, picking up the enamel pail before heading for the byre and the milking.

At six on the dot I met the men in the farm close on the way to the house for breakfast. I had set the table the night before—a large bowl filled with oatmeal, salt and pepper; two small bowls at each setting—usually white with blue stripes—one for milk, the other for each worker to make his own brose. The bowls were filled with fresh milk from the last milking the previous night. Thick slices of plain bread, one for each person, were placed on a round wooden breadboard beside the butter and syrup. The black iron kettle would be at the boil, hanging from the crook of the swy. A large blue enamel teapot sat on the binkie by the peat fire. Dinner was served before noon at eleven-thirty, the main meal of the day. A typical meal was tattie soup, hard fish and mustard sauce with chappit tatties, and most likely a milk pudding—rice, sago or semolina, which had been boiled in a three-legged iron pot with a bow handle. Pan loaf, butter and jam would be laid on the table at tea-time, and, of course, oatcakes. The men might also have a plate of saps, with a few raisins thrown in, and perhaps a boiled egg, or cheese. Now and then we had yellow fish, cooked on a wire contraption over red 'quiles' (similar to the barbecue method we know today).

While the men were at breakfast I would be in the byre milking the cows, sitting on my three-legged wooden stool. Grandma would join me later to milk her cow, a pedigree Shorthorn, the last surviving animal of her late father's prize herd. Grandma would press her head into the warm flank of the cow who was chewing the cud contentedly, then there would be silence for a while except for the sound of warm rich milk gushing into the pail. 'It's the promise o' a fine hairst day' says grandma, 'Ye'll likely be needed at the forkin!'

I glanced down at the palms of my hands already blistered from the friction of the fork shaft of the previous day. I had been told they'd harden as the harvest progressed. An extra pair of hands was always needed at hairst time, usually for forkin' the sheaves on to the carts pulled by willing and hard-working Clydesdales. Building the sheaves on to the carts required considerable skill. Extra wooden shelves were fixed on to the sides to hold a wider and higher load. If the load wasn't properly built, it would be in danger of slipping off on its way to the cornyard, builder and all!

Piece-time was aye a welcome break, brought by grandma in a large sturdy basket. A bottle or two of home-made raspberry wine would be included as an extra—sheer nectar to slake our thirst after hours of toiling in the hot sun. A flagon of tea as well, and golden girdle scones flavoured with the tang of peat reek, and spread with rich yellow butter and blackcurrant jam!

The men slept in the chaumer which was part of the farm steading. In winter a fire was lit, as they spent their evenings there. The beds were covered in heavy patchwork quilts, and underneath, a few crocheted blankets. On the floor by the fireplace was spread a clootie rug—all these made by the womenfolk during the dark winter evenings. The only furniture was a few chairs and the kists belonging to the fee'd men, which held their clothes and meagre possessions.

After the men finished their supper (as tea-time was referred to then) they each in turn had a wash in the back scullery, the water being carried from a wooden pump at the back of the cornyard, about a hundred yards from the farmhouse. An inch or two of water was taken in one of the pails to prime the pump.

In an evening, perhaps the workers from a neighbouring farm would come over to our barn and have a game of pitch-and-toss on the stone floor, or maybe they would vie with each other in feats of strength. On winter nights they would bring along their melodeons, fiddles, jews harps and mouth-organs, and through the open chaumer windows, in the peace of the frosty air, would flow the couthie music of the old bothy ballads of Buchan.

GLADYS M WATSON

Peasant

As I gaed doon by the Village Square
I spied twa loons in a fecht,
"Ye peasant!", ane cried as the neives swung roon,
An' the battle reached its hicht.

"Na! Na!" I thocht as they strove awa'
"I doot ye maun be wrang,
Tho' ye think that noo, ma smairt wee loon
Ye'll ken it's nae richt e'er lang."

For a peasant's a chiel wi' the Earth in his bleed,
Haunds blistered wi' tchavin' at wark,
A lad wha smiles thro' the mist an' rain
An' the holes in his weel-worn sark.

He disna bend tae gentry fowk
Like the wind-blawn corn in his park
Frae the mists o' Time, he gangs doon wi' the sun,
An gets yokit in tune wi' the lark.

The sweit on his brow frae age tae age
Has filled the hale World's plate,
As the years gang by, he carries his load
In his weary an' shufflin' gait.

Sae, loon, dinna scorn the chiel wha kens
The meanin' o' workin' the soil,
For the fare that *ye* hae for ilka day
Is the price o' the peasant's toil.

GILLESPIE D MUNRO

To A Long-Departed Crofter

(on finding his abandoned croft, Braidshaw,
 up an old Upper Cabrach road)

You have been long gone now.
I know not who you were,
But yet I greet you.
The parks you wrested from the heather
Are a rustling memorial still
To your endeavour.
But these vacant rigs that knew your plough,
Saw your strong arms and sturdy tread,
Are starting to forget.
The heather's creeping back.

You have been long gone now.
Your home's but a pile of stones.
Your dykes are down.
The burn still spills by the drystone walls,
But the trees are dying and dead,
As the old life has died.
Only shooting parties halt here now
With pâté sandwiches and flask:
Cartridges strew the floor.
The heather's creeping back.

You have been long gone now.
Forgive me if I pause and muse,
Let out a sigh.
Here, in a harsh land, you carved a home,
Lived a hard and unpretentious life:
You played your part.
Unlike these winds that about us blow,
You were a prisoner of your time,
As I am of mine.
The heather's creeping back.

You have been long gone now.
In the course of my cluttered life
I pause and view.

Time must have meant little here.
Days would pass, seasons come and go,
And so did you.
We each have to plough our furrow
And raise up our heaps of stones,
Return to our beginnings.
The heather's creeping back.

MICHAEL G KIDD

The Turra Shelt

"Aye there's fairly changes takin' place jist noo." 'At wiz fit ma freen Geordie Will said at the mart the day, an' he's nae half right. Noo fan ye tak' a wander oot oor back door ye can see six, seven different fairms. Weel there's naething new aboot 'at like. They've a' been 'ere since ma granfaither wiz a loon, if nae langer, bit at's nae the thing. Ye see maist o' the folk in 'em are a' foreigners.

O' aye they've a' traiked up fae a' bits o' the country t' this neuk, bringin' beests an' bairns alike, an' a great lot o' ideas an' funny wyes o' spikkin'. Jings, ye dinna half hiv a job catchin' their twang at times. If it carries on like this though, ye'll seen be sair made t' fin' a weel kint face. Of coorse there's aye been een or twa strangers that hiv come t' bide here, like yon lad Crowther. Aye there's still a puckle folk roon here than ken the story o' Jimmie Morrison an' his neighbour . . .

A rare smile cam' ower Jimmie Morrison's face (or Knowie as folks ca'ed him, seein' he bid at Knowbrae) as he looked up eence again at the raws o' rosettes lined up alang the stable wa'. He stepped a bit closer t' blaw a bit stue aff een, for Knowie wiz as prood o' they ribbons as the fussiest hoosewife wi' her best china. Ye see, winnin' rosettes hid a lang tradition at Knowbrae.

It a' started lang seen wi' aul' Knowie fa hid won a couple o' shows roon aboot wi' his shelts. Takin' aff his faither Tam Morrison, Knowie hid teen tae the shelts as weel, an' hid deen his bit tae keep up the name his faither hid started afore him. Noo it wiz Knowie's turn, an' he'd be damned if things were gan tae change in his day. Sae it wiz there were still a couple o' shelts gan aboot at Knowbrae.

Noo his faither hid aye been kint as bein' a bit grippy, bit folks said Knowie wiz worse; aye it wisna' aften the mochs got oot o' his wallet they said. Still fan it came tae horses, Knowie wiz niver a lad tae be ticht wi' money, feeds fu' o' molasses an' linseed, braw lookin' leather, even the odd vet's bill, Knowie wid fork oot fit iver it took tae keep his shelts first class. Monie's the body that's thocht if he spent half as much time or money on yon dour, skinny crater o' a wife o' his, she might be mair ready wi' a smile or freenly word instead o' yon affy glour ye got ilka time ye saw her at the kirk.

Knowie still wi 'an ee on the rosettes caught sicht o' the word Turriff Show. "Turra show" he said to himsel' and that rare squint kin' o' smile stretched still further fae ae lug till the ither, till the hale o' Knowie's face contorted wi' a great grin o' satisfaction, like a cat that's got her share o' the cream. Knowbrae hid been takin' first prize for shelts at Turra for years noo, an' thinkin' o' Dobbin oot 'ere in the park, Knowie hid nae reason to see why things should be ony different the morn.

Takin' a puff o' his pipe, Knowie went ower the coort, by the byre, till he cam tae the park, far this year's hope for Turra stood chaain' awa at some girse. Sendin' cloods o' rick ti swirl roon his bonnet, Knowie took anither puff o' his pipe an' hid a guid look ower his shelt. She wiz a braw beast. Dobbin, or as she wiz kint in the show ring, Knowbrae Diamond (for the maisters at Knowbrae hid aye prided themsels on haein' a fancy name for their shelts) wiz prize winnin' stuff, Knowie wiz sure o' it. Lookin' at the fine structured, sturdy body, the shapely legs wi' their sloppin' pasterns and neat roonded hooves, the lang black mane that shone like a polished bawbee, Knowie, fa hid groomed the shelt ilka mornin' for months felt a rush o' pride at the result o' a' his handiwork.

Jist then Knowie's wave o' ecstasy wiz interrupted by the soun' o' a tractor coming up ower the brae. The perpetrator o' this din wiz Knowie's neighbour, Crowther. Naebody kint much aboot the lang streak o' a man; some said he hailed fae Edinburgh, others thocht he belonged tae the Borders. He'd boucht Mains O' Cairntoul a couple o' months back, an' as the hale business had been raither quick, word went aboot that there wiz some sort o' fishy business aboot the sale o' his last fairm. Davie Gorse, fa wiz aye a bit o' a blether, hid telt a'body at the mart he'd been bankrupt, but ithers like Lizzie Smith o' the village shop, fa hid her nose pit oot o' jint fan Crowther hid telt her things seemed tae be dearer in this pairt o' the country, wiz sure he'd been on some sort o' tax fiddle. Knowie, fa wisna much interested in the gossip spread aboot by aul' wives like Lizzie Smith, didna gie much thocht tae his neighbours' past, still that wisna tae say he didnae hae his doots about him. Knowie, a man o' fyowe words himsel' hidna said mair than a couple o' utterances, let alone hid he heen a guid claik wi' his neighbour; yet fae these brief exchanges, Knowie could tell there wiz somethin' aboot him.

Knowie minded the wye he wid look at ye wi' yon black een o' his, a' the time wi' a smirk on his face as if he kint somethin' you didnae. Bit at wisna a'. A couple o' months back fan Knowie hid been oot near ilka nicht wi' his lambs, he'd seem somebody sleekin' aboot in the middle o' the nicht. The lang, bony figure that hid appeared oot o' the darkness meant there wiz nae mistakin', it wiz Crowther a'richt.

Suddenly Knowie spluttered ower his pipe, "Crowther, jings why did I nae think o' him afore." Knowie's complexion turned fyte, a' the smugness bein' fair drained oot o' it as he looked ower the neep parks tae the grun o' Mains O' Cairntoul. Twa black shelts were careering about fu' o' high jinks. "Twa black shelts that could tak' a prize at Turra," thought Knowie, his belly fair churnin' at the idea. He hidnae felt sae nae weel since yon day the wife hid kicked up sic a soun', he'd agreed tae buy her a new frock in Markies only tae fin' he'd lost his wallet.

After a lang days chav Knowie kicked aff his wellies, leavin' 'em sprawlin' ower the doorstep and gave the barometer a chap as usual. Weel it promised tae be a fine day, yet it didnae dae much tae lift Knowie's spirits: it wiz time for stronger stuff. Helpin' himsel' tae a dram, Knowie did a mental check. Aye a'thing wiz in order, Dobbin wiz in the stable so there'd be nae chance o' her bein' a' mucky for the big day, the leather had been polished tul ye could see ye're face in it, he'd phoned Wullie Scott for a float, an' the missus hid washed and pressed his ain claithes. It wisna often Knowie took much bother ower his appearance; the wife wiz sair made tae get him t' wear a suit for a weddin' or funeral. Still show days were show days an' there wiz standards tae be kept. Yet that nicht as Knowie climbed the stairs, his face a bit flushed fae the fuskie bottle, his mind wiz still on the twa shelts at Mains O' Cairntoul. If only he kint if they were gan tae be at the show or no!

Next mornin' at the crack o' dawn Knowie wiz suppin' at his brose bowl—nae that he'd much o' an appetite; he'd hardly slept a' nicht for the thocht o' the twa beasts ower the parks. A'body kint Knowbrae hid been first prize for the shelts' class for years, bit fit if it didna 'is time? Still 'at wiz nae wye tae be thinkin', there wiz a lot o' work yet tae be deen. Pullin' his bonnet ower his baldy pow Knowie went oot the back door ready tae get yokin'. But fit a sicht met him; there flappin' open in the early mornin' breeze wiz the stable door. Inside it wiz empty.

For a minute, fair mesmerised, Knowie stottered aboot in the coort as if he'd been at the bottle, then comin' back tae his senses he ran ower tae the stable. Aye there wiz nae mistakin', Dobbin wiz gone. His heart thumpin' like a thrashin' mull Knowie ran tae the byre, bit there wiz nae sign o' Dobbin 'ere, nor in the feed shed or ony ither o' the buildings at Knowhead.

Fair in a swyte wi' himsel' Knowie ran up tae the tap o' the hull at the back o' the hoose. He'd seen hae a gran view o' the countryside fae up there, surely he'd see Dobbin then. Yet, though he could tell fa wiz nae lang up for miles aroon gan' be the rick yoamin' oot o' their lums, Dobbin wiz nae wye tae be seen. Jist then Knowie looked ower the wye o' Mains

O' Cairntoul, "That wiz it, Crowther wiz feart o' the competition, he'd pinched Dobbin."

Knowie, fa hid never been sae worked up in a' his life wiz takin' teerin' doon the hull like a bull on the rampage. Dreepin' in swyte Knowie made stricht for Mains O' Cairntoul, cursin' a' the fyle. "O' a' the mean tricks! It looked as if Lizzie Smith wiz richt after a'. Well, he need nae think he'll get aff wi' it," thought Knowie grittin' his falsers thegither.

Reed in the face, an' nae far aff a hert attack, Knowie wiz comin' beltin' up the road tae Cairntoul. Pechin' like an aul' dog, Knowie stopped for a minute tae get his win' back an' jist aboot fell ower, fan there in broad daylicht wiz Crowther, a rope in his hand wi' Dobbin at the ither end o' it. There wiz nae stoppin' Knowie noo.

Grabbin' a graip that wiz lyin' at the side o' the road, Knowie wiz in nae mind for ony nonsense! "Hey min" he cried near chokin' himsel' as the bleed wint racin' roon his body. "Fit dae ye think ye're daein' wi' ma shelt?"

Crowther, fa looked fair dumbfounded at the affy sicht o' Knowie brandishin' the graip like a man geen gyte, tee say a word. Knowie carried on rantin' an' ravin'. "Ye de'il, I'll hae the polis on tae 'es, jist ye wyte, the bobbies will hae ye locked up Crowther, ye'll nae get aff, I'll get ye."

"Now just a minute, I'll have the police on to you," cried back Crowther, still haudin' on tae Dobbin an' dancin' a sort o'Highland Fling at the same time as he dodged the prongs o' the graip. Fair stuck at this impudence Knowie seemed tae turn a queer shade o' blue an' wiz jist aboot tae come oot wi' somethin' else fan Crowther spat oot, "Now look here Mr Morrison, I think there's been some sort of a mistake."

"Ye look here, there's nae mistak' aboot it, you've pinched ma shelt an' I can prove it."

"That's just it. I haven't stolen your pony, if anything I've saved her life."

"Ye've fit?" cried Knowie a look o' confusion comin' ower his face.

"Yes, you see last night I was looking for some badgers—it's my hobby. I discovered a sett by the edge of the woods a few months ago. Anyway, on my way back I heard a neighing sound. When I went to investigate I saw it was your pony on that bit of waste land eating ragwort to her heart's content. Well I know a thing or two about ponies myself. I've got two of my friends' in livery at the moment. If I'd left her to her own devices she could easily have poisoned herself. As it is she seems to be none the worse today. I was just about to return her when you turned up."

Bye noo Knowie wiz standin' still haudin' the graip an' lookin' gye sheepish, his heid facin' his wellies. Takin' Dobbin fae Crowther he looked up at his neighbour an' mumbled "I'm sorry, I must hiv forgotten tae sneck the stable door last night. It's jist that it's Turra Show the day an' I'm a bit excited, ye see." Wi' 'at Knowie an' Dobbin traichled back tae Knowbrae, a gye bit slower than the wye he'd cam', for fit wi' a' the rinnin' aboot Knowie's rheumatics were gaein' him gip.

Weel in spite o' a' the consternation that 'ear Knowbrae Diamond took the reed rosette at Turra, ensuring Knowie o' anither ribbon for the stable wa', his name in the *P & J* an' the praise o' like minded lads fae near an' far. Yet somehoo Knowie's takin' the first prize that 'ear didnae seem tae interest folks as much as usual. Ye see they were tae witness somethin' far mair rare. That afterneen fan the sun wiz kickin' up a great heat tae mak abody plooter an' rin for the beer tent, the company githered were tae see somethin' nae short o' a miracle. Sprawled ower the beer coonter, wallet lyin' for a' tae see, wiz Knowie o' Knowbrae buyin' his neighbour, the new lad Crowther, a pint.

MORAG FARQUHAR

Bogton

To a child raised in the town, the farm buildings were a source of endless mystery and adventure. The byre, even when the beasts were out in the parks, was full of the aromas euphemistically referred to by townies as "country smells". There was comfort in the smells that lingered there, and come winter, when the beasts were taken in, there were the calves, timid and gangly, for a timid, gangly child to wonder at.

Memories stay with me of the warm, sweet breath that steamed from their velvety nostrils when they trusted me enough to sidle gingerly up to me; of their huge eyes, trying to understand this strange animal that walked on two legs instead of four; of the heifers, keeping a watchful eye on proceedings and lowing nervously.

Next door, a stone shed harboured an immense collection of agricultural detritus. The walls were covered with an astonishing array of harness recalling the golden age of horsepower: vast leather yokes, cracked reins and ancient bits, hung up on their nails at the end of their last day's work years before, and untouched since.

Every surface was inches deep in a miscellany of objects accumulated over decades of farming: broken, rusty implements put away until time could be found to mend them; rudely fashioned home-made tools which bore witness to the thrift and improvisation of generations of farmers;

lethal-looking contraptions whose unspeakable veterinary purposes could only be guessed at, and which a child's over-active imagination pictured all too vividly as instruments of torture.

Across the yard was a lean-to shed, open on two sides, which housed the larger farm machinery. Two elderly tractors and a variety of bogeys were its principal occupants, and of these, naturally, the tractors were the greater attraction. Both were vintage Massey Fergusons which had seen better days, and which appeared to break down with monotonous regularity at the most inopportune moments. Every October we would all converge on Bogton to "lift the tatties", and every October the tractor would break down before it reached the end of the first drill, occasioning the first of a series of increasingly desperate running repairs. Stationary and silent, though, in the tractor shed, they were make-believe tanks and planes and submarines and racing cars—powerful, reassuring and perfect.

Behind the byre was an area of open ground littered with rusty, long-discarded implements and carts which made ideal nests for wayward poultry which stubbornly refused to lay where they were supposed to. I used to be charged every day of the holidays with the task of searching out their secret hiding places and raiding the eggs: thirty years later I can still remember the most favoured locations!

Overlooking this yard, and reached by means of an external wooden staircase, was a grain store where the summer's bounty was laid out and dried before being bagged and dispatched. The hairst was my favourite time of year at Bogton. My sister and I, too young to be of any help in the operation, must have been little more than a liability, but I don't recall ever being made aware of it. We would lie in the bogey as my uncle, driving the tractor which pulled it, drew alongside the combine harvester and the crop began to cascade down on top of us. We shrieked with delight and that pleasurable state of barely-suppressed panic as the heavy grain engulfed us, waiting until the last possible moment before struggling free. And then the ride back to the farm yard, lying on our backs on top of the mountain of grain and gazing up at endless, open skies until it was time for the contents of the bogey to be tipped on to the elevator that lifted it to the store.

Sharing a mutual wall with the tractor shed was what had once been the dairy, where my grandmother had spent a lifetime labouring over a churn and pans which she had kept gleaming clean, but which I recall only as dull shadows of their former glory. Their tarnished appearance notwithstanding, however, it all seemed to me at the time as if my grandmother had just gone out for the day and would be coming back tomorrow to pick up where she had left off. Skimming ladles and butter pats lay where she had put them down years before, and I remember playing with the churn but tiring very quickly, and wondering how she could have kept turning it long enough to transform cream into butter.

I remember too being told about the time when as a child my uncle, sent to deliver butter to the village one hot day in summer, had a puncture on his bike when he had gone three-quarters of the way, and instead of continuing on foot to complete the errand, returned home consumed with concern for the stricken bike, with the butter dripping from its greaseproof wrapper in the pannier. The telling-off he received must have been a memorable one, for he could still recount the story sixty years later.

A collection of ramshackle henhouses, home to a collection of ramshackle poultry, stood in the shade of a small copse of trees just behind the farmhouse. A massive chestnut, overgrown with ivy, dominated the others and was my favourite climbing tree. Two rowans, a couple of conifers of indeterminate species and an ancient stump—the remains of another once mighty chestnut tree struck by lightning years before—completed the ensemble. There was besides, just in front of the house, a cherry tree which fruited prodigiously for decades until it too fell victim to lightning. It was split in two one stormy January night and remained for years a mute, dead testament of the awesome powers of nature, until comparatively recently when gale-force winds completed the destruction begun years before.

The house itself was large and cold, with many rooms which were reserved for special occasions or otherwise out of use. A Raeburn stove heated the small kitchen which was the heart of the house, emitting a fierce but uncontrollable heat which had once been responsible for incinerating one of my uncle's best shirts. Hung over the rail to dry overnight, all that remained of it in the morning were six mother-of-pearl buttons in the hearth.

A long, gloomy passage led from the kitchen to the front door of the house, which I never saw used in all the time I was a regular visitor to Bogton. The wall at the far end of the passage from the kitchen door was adorned with the stuffed head of a prize ram, who in life had been possessed of a magnificent pair of curly horns and a roguish disposition. In death, to a small child, he was a source of enduring terror. I would find any excuse not to walk down the corridor alone, and even when accompanied, and feigning indifference, I was transfixed by the steely gaze of his cold, unseeing eyes.

On either side of the front door were large reception rooms funished with Victorian sofas, jardinieres, mahogany sideboards and Sunday-best anti-macassars. One boasted a piano, lamentably out of tune, and a handsome black marble fireplace. An unusual arrangement of two staircases one at each end of the house led to two sets of rooms upstairs, which were uniformly small and cosy but not directly accessible one from the other.

The overhanging landing on the front stair was a little too low for anyone of above average height to descend the stair comfortably, and my grandmother, who descended it every day for more than sixty years, was in the habit of putting up a hand to steady herself as she ducked her head. Over the years, the repeated touch of her hand on the same spot wore away the varnish and eventually left a smooth depression in the woodwork: it's a source of abiding regret to me that the new owners who moved in when the farm was finally sold last year will never know the reason for that worn patch in the woodwork, and will probably have painted over it without a second thought.

IAN GILL

Home-Produced

My parents went to a croft in the Hills of Fisherie in May 1919, a few months after I was born, and it was there I was brought up. At the age of five I went to the two-roomed Upperbrae school (now a farm implement shed), and stayed there until I was twelve. This meant a four mile walk every day. When I finished at Upperbrae I had to go to Crudie school, also more than four miles from home.

In those days there were no school buses; I wonder what the children of today would say if they were told to walk eight miles to school and back. In the winter time we only saw home in daylight on Saturday and Sunday: were away before daylight and it was dark by the time we returned—but I was never absent, and was never late. I was blessed with good health, (though I would have got First Prize for sore feet!) and I was glad to leave school at the early age of 13½ years.

When my father paid one of his first visits to Turra Mart in the spring he would bring home two young pigs. For the first few days they were very unhappy having just been taken away from their mother, and screamed and squealed their heads off. I suppose, like human beings, they missed a mother's love. But what a pleasure they were to us for a while after they settled down. All summer we fed them, until they fattened out and were nice and plump, knowing full well that some day they would be killed (a necessary evil) to help us feed ourselves in winter. One was sold to Mr Grant, the butcher in Gardenstown, the other was killed at home. A neighbour Jimmy Chalmers, who was also a butcher, performed this dreadful task, cleaned the pig and cut it up for us. There were no freezers in those days and since pork did not keep in good condition for very long, we sold some of it to the surrounding neighbours.

We were never told which day the killing would happen, but we always found out because on that day the pigs were given no breakfast, only a drink of water, a task which often fell to me. I remember standing looking at them for the last time, my eyes brimming with tears, thinking how cruel human beings could be, at the same time vowing I would never eat another bite of pork or bacon. I'm afraid this vow was short lived however! When I smelled bacon frying, pea soup boiling, or a piece of pork roasting, the smell would go round my heart like a hairy worm and I'd dive in with the rest of the family when it was served up, forgetting I was eating one of those loveable animals I had so often cleaned out, fed and had fun with.

When it was time to make Mealie Jimmies it was from Jimmy Chalmers that we got the skins which were sheep guts. This meant a lot of work for my mother. First the skin had to be soaked in salt and water for a few days, then washed and scrubbed with a soft brush on both sides. Turning them over was a tricky business; we pushed them on to a spurtle, taking hold of the edge and quickly flipping it back. After this was all done to my mother's satisfaction, she prepared the mixture for filling them—oatmeal, finely chopped onions, salt and pepper and roast fat—all mixed together in a big bowl. The skins were then put on to a fairly big funnel, and mixture poured and pushed down into them, using a finer spurtle. The skins were then tied with string every four or five inches, not forgetting a twist first, to stop them from opening up while boiling, which was the final step.

DAVINA S WATSON

Winter Housekeeping

The Hills of Fisherie is a rather remote area in north-east Aberdeenshire and on the border of Banffshire, well known for very stormy weather in winter, which often arrives early and stays late. I remember some years having roads blocked with snow for nine or ten weeks. When this happened no vans (which we depended on) could get through with provisions. If we did run out of essentials, my father and some of the neighbours would take a horse and sledge and go to Gardenstown, New Byth, or even Turriff, to stock up the larders.

To avoid this if possible, my mother would always try to have a good store of non-perishable foods. In the summertime she made lots of jam—rhubarb, gooseberry, strawberry, blackcurrant, and apple and redcurrant jelly—all from fruit grown in our own garden. There were about 5 acres of heather on the croft then on which grew blaeberries and wild red and yellow rasps. These too were gathered and made into jam. The blaeberries were a slow, tedious pick and they were so small it took a long time to fill a two pound jar. Sure enough, when the jar was almost full and not very securely placed on the ground, it would tip over and the berries would be lost in the long heather! My mother's jams always turned out delicious, firm and well jellied. She needed no recipe book to guide her, but one of her secrets was that she would only make jam with fruit picked on a dry day.

Next to be found in mother's winter store were whole dried salted cod, bought from a fish house in Gardenstown. What a lovely supper they made, boiled and served with mustard sauce and mashed potatoes. Left overs were used to make hairy tatties next day, another good substantial meal, eaten with oal. cakes and washed down with a glass of milk. There was also a barrel of salt herrings which was kept outside because of the strong smell. The barrel used to get frozen over and we had to use a mallet to break the ice to get the herrings out. They made another satisfying meal, boiled on top of the tatties left in their jackets. Mind you, they didn't half raise a thirst, so usually this meal was left as near to bedtime as possible, so we would not have to get up during the night after drinking too much water!

Oatmeal was made from the oats grown on the croft. The nearest meal mill was at Craigston, quite a few miles away, so it took my father practically a whole day to go there and get this job done. He would fill up the cart with sacks of oats and be away by 6 a.m. Some oats he got bruised down for cattle feed; the rest was made into oatmeal. After the meal was made, you were left with sids and dust which was mixed into the hens' feed. Some of the sids (which is the hard shell of the oats) was soaked in a barrel of water, left for a week or two to ferment, then strained off and bottled; this was called Sowens. When required, it was boiled and could be flavoured with salt or sugar. As children we preferred sugar, and we often had this at bedtime—a great nightcap.

Milk became scare in the winter, so mother always made Watson's tonic stout. I don't know if it's still on the market—I haven't seen it in years and have forgotten how it was made; but I remember she kept it in a barrel two or three weeks after making it, before bottling it. Even then, the corks would pop off or, if they were too tight, the bottom of the bottle would blow out—and then there was a bonnie mess to clean up!

DAVINA S WATSON

Cheese-Making

My mother also made cheese during the summer months when milk was more plentiful. There were two kinds, first sweet-milk, which was best, made with the milk just as it came from the cow before the cream was taken off; and a second, stronger in taste, made with the milk after the cream had been taken out. We owned no separator, so it meant the milk had to stand a day or two in earthenware basins until the cream rose to the top, to be skimmed off and made into butter.

For cheesemaking the milk had to be heated up in a pot, then some rennet was stirred in to curdle the milk which was left standing for a while, the whey being poured off from time to time. Then, when the milk was a solid mass, it was removed from the pot and kept in a strainer until enough was collected, sufficient to a cheese.

For many years my mother used her hands (which would be frowned upon and considered unhygienic today) to break up the solid masses and mix in salt. Later on, she got a mincer, which was a great time-saver. When the mixture was all broken up and rubbed down to a smooth consistency, it was ready to be put into the chessil, a small wooden barrel with many holes in the bottom and round the sides, to allow the remaining whey to drain off, under pressure, when put into the cheese press. First a square of cheese cloth was put into the chessil, followed by the mixture, which was pressed well down. When full, the lid which fitted inside the chessil was put on and it was ready to be put into the cheese press, where it would remain for a day or two, under pressure, until all the whey was drained off. Then it was taken out of the chessil and left in the sun to dry off before being stored away.

We sold cheese, butter and eggs in Gardenstown every Saturday. Most of the crofters did likewise, each having their own customers. We all got a better price for our goods there than if we had sold to the vans. My father, when he had time, would go there too on Saturday, selling peats, sticks, potatoes, turnips, carrots, cabbage and leeks. I had to accompany him, going round the houses collecting orders, then staying by the horse and cart while he delivered. Every penny counted.

DAVINA S WATSON

The Neep

A neep wis lyin' in a field
Een' bricht n' sunny day
Fin ower' come a muckle coo
Fair stapit up wi hay

Ses coo—"You look a tasty neep
      Shiny, fat n' bonny"
      "Oh no am' nae"—the neep speared oot
      "Ah'm really wee n' scrawny"

      "Ah' think you'll dee me fine yi ken,
      Ah've hid my fu' o' kale—
      Now will I crunch yi' inti bits—
      Or will I gulp yi hale?"

      "Hae peety muckle coo—I'm sure
      Your belly is quite full—
      Di'yi ken yi've an admirer in
      Yon black n' brawny bull?"

Wi that the coo gid oot a glunce—
N' richt enough of a'
A bonny bit o' Angus wis fair
HINGIN o'er i wa!

      "Yi see—I telt yi—" said the neep
      In hushed and sleekit tones
      "The ways he's lookin it yi—
      Dis it nae jist bile yer bones?!"

      "At's true fine neep" the coo replied
      "I'll let him dee his wurst
      Bit afore I ging aff courtin' him
      I'm gan ti eat you first!"

GAIL A WALKER

The Auld Fairm Haun'

Doon by the briggie auld Doddie reminisces
Aboot times o' lang syne an' a' the things he misses
He thinks real fairm work's deen a nonsense ower fast
Spring times an' the grubber, are a' things o' the past.

Fegs, there's nae time noo for delvin' in the neuks
Fairm chiels noo-a-days they learn it a' fae beuks
Ye nivver hear 'em singin' at the harra or the ploo
Their lugs are either happit up or stuffed wi' cotton 'oo.

There's nae mare stibble ruckies, or dollies made wi' corn,
A great machine gaes thrashin' a' an's lookit at wi' scorn
Machines for liftin' tatties—aye an' pu'in' neeps as weel
Sure's ocht there's nae wark noo for the ordinar' fairm chiel.

The clatter o' the hames an' theats wis music tae the ear
An' the horses' lugs they cockit fan lousin' time drew near,
I s'pose it a' means progress, they wey things a' are gyan,
Bit fegs! It's hard tae tak' in by an aul' fairm haun'.

MARGARET GREIG

Chores

I would like to think I did help my mother a little before or after school. I
milked a cow before I went to school in the morning for a spell while she
was unwell and scrubbed a pig (we kept two) the night before it went to
market. I scrubbed it with an old-fashioned scrubbing brush. Mr Gibb,
who owned the shoemakers shop in Tarves used to come round the
countryside taking orders for footwear and my mother would say "If the
pig fetches a good price you'll get new shoes."

Whether the beautifully scrubbed pig went for a higher price I never
really knew, but I always got my shoes!

MOLLY CRAIG

Tattie Picking

And then there was the tattie pickin'. It was a great honour to be picked for a tattie squad. A fortnight of extremely hard graft, and as far as I recall, high pay—two guineas a day! Slave labour some would call it nowadays for the work is back breaking, but to us it was a great adventure—picked up on a dark, cold, autumn morning by the bogie and transported to a field miles away in the middle of nowhere, with your flask and piece. In fact the field was probably about a mile from home! Nevertheless having survived the shame of holding up the digger at some point you were given a vast sum of money at the end of the week and were let loose, to spend your hard-won gains. I remember being able to afford a box of 2/11*d*. fireworks for bonfire night, so the tattie holidays must have been relatively late that year!

J McLEISH

A Buchan Childhood

Growing up on our small farm in the days before automation was idyllic for a child not really required to work. I sat on the 'step' of the binder, helped to take the tea and scones to the workers, and sat on the coles of hay while the horses dragged them to the farmyard. My cousin and I played in the moss, acres of it, and made our houses in the heather. There was always a bit of magic in the moss. What a disappointment to discover when I returned years later that it had been reclaimed and was just part of the new farmer's ordinary field.

School life was fairly uneventful apart from my running away when I was moved to 'Higher Infants' and thought I couldn't do the sums. I recall meeting one of the lady farmers as I walked that mile home with my head down, and I was barely there when my big brother aged 13 (and a very angry brother at that!) burst in. The dominie had sent him to fetch me!

A mile long walk in rutted farm roads, dusty in summer, 'dubby' in winter. On getting to school in winter we would swing our arms from the shoulders to restore circulation, the boys more manfully clapping their arms across their chests. We had to walk through a field which, although it was a Right of Way, was full of cattle in summer, but we were never afraid of stirks dashing towards us as we knew there was no bull among them. Lumps of rock salt lay on the ground and we'd go up and have a 'sook'—we never worried about germs! As thermos flasks hadn't reached

our corner then we took enamel flasks to school, which we were allowed
to put by the coal fire in the classroom—and of course we had a 'piece'. I
didn't care for home-made cheese so mine was just jam most days. A boy
who sat beside me for a time had a syrup piece, without butter or
margarine, and I can recall to this day the sickening smell of that plain
loaf!

MOLLY CRAIG

Laundress

Perhaps the final link with my bothying days was severed with the death
of a very old lady last May. She was a ploughman's wife who for a number
of my bothy years did my washing. I often marvelled at the excellence of
the semi-stiff collars and shirt fronts which she was able to produce in the
most primitive of circumstances. The cottage had only a living room and a
bedroom. Water was carried from a spring about a hundred yards from
the cottage and washing done in the open in a tub, while whites were
boiled in a 'witches pot' over a brick brazier.

I always knew that she did not labour over her tub for the pittance I was
able to offer, but that the spotless shirts were a product of her warm heart,
and her concern for a boy living away from home.

IAN C THOMSON

Snowstorm

It had been a beautiful morning that day towards the end of 1911 or 1912
when two companions and I set off by bicycle for Fyvie School, about four
and a half miles from home. There was not a breath of wind or any cloud
in the sky, but towards mid-day the wind rose suddenly bringing snow.
The force of the wind increased and the roads were soon 'filling up'. The
headmaster decided that the 'long distance' pupils should go home, so at
2 p.m. we set off to face gale-force winds and drifting snow. We should
have left our bicycles as they were of no use to us, just adding to our
burden, but we struggled on to within one and a half miles of home at
which point we decided we could go no further and prepared to sit down
by the roadside. Fortunately at that moment the farmer of Macternay
passed with horse and milk cart on his way home from Fyvie Station

where he had delivered a consignment of milk for Aberdeen. After 80 years I can hear him yet saying to us "C'mon noo lassies, dinna sit doon there. Get intae my tracks". We did so and when we came to the farm, he awaited us. "Pit yer bikes intae this shed an' come intae the hoose. There's a cup o' tey for ye". We were like snowmen (or women)! Our coats were frozen hard and we could not sit down. But we were very grateful for the tea which refreshed us. Then the farmer said "Noo, I'm pittin' ye intae this park. Ye see that palin', haud on tae it and dinna let go. Ye ken far ye'll come oot". We couldn't *see* the paling—it was 'blin' smorr' but we held on to it. Actually, we were traversing the base of a triangle, and soon after we joined the main road we met my father on his way to look for us. A few yards farther on the brother of one of my companions was on the same mission. We did not see our bicycles again for three weeks and had to walk to and from school every day!

BARBARA J WATSON

Parliamentary Language

Just before the war, when there was a Bill before Parliament to increase farm workers wages, a farmer friend showed me a cutting from Hansard in which the Honourable Member for Banffshire pleaded for the Bill to be thrown out, claiming that if it were to go through, most of Banffshire's farmers would go bankrupt. He claimed also that his farmers fed their men well. When asked "With what?" he replied that four herrings and tatties was their main meal, adding that, as a matter of fact, he himself ate four herrings daily. There was laughter in the House when a wag asked him what he had besides the four herrings. There was no reply.

My farmer friend's reaction to the cutting was that the Honourable Member must have been joking: everyone knew that a farmworker's main meal was neep brose!

W B LUCIA

FOLK

The Duffer

Different folks leave different impressions on a body as they journey through life, but I think the ghost o' Mrs McArthur lies maist deeply imbedded in *my* psyche. Fifty years on an' I still get the odd feelin' that maybe she had second sight.

I nivver kent her man's first name, he was jist Aul' McArthur, but the pair o' them hid retired oot o' the ferm and cam' tae bide in the hoosie next door. Gran' neighbours they were tae and my folks seemed tae get on weel wi' them. On the occasion that has since made me think that Mrs McArthur had some kind of visionary powers I kent that the fower o' them were gaun awa' for a run in the car. I heard the Chrysler startin' up and ran roon' the corner o' the hoose tae say cheerio tae them. I trippit as I ran and gaed a' ma length in the close, skinned ma knees and tore ma breeks. I wis only a wee loon and I grat, my knees were that sair. My mither got oot o' the car tae dry ma een an' dicht me doon. Mrs McArthur jist sat in the back o' the car an' said, "Ach Donal', I doot ye'll aye be a bit o' a duffer." She was really a kindly aul' body, there wis sympathy in her voice; bit mony a time since, when things ha'e gaen wrang for me, her words have echoed doon through the years.

A few years after that I was big enough tae go a bike. My father had started a sma' business jist aboot the time that I was born. He put in the village's first petrol pump, opened a wee shoppie, sortit bikes and wirelesses, ran a hirin' car and in 1942 got the Post Office. He sell't new bikes as weel, an' of coorse he wid tak' back an aul' machine in part exchange. It was ane o' them that I landed wi'. It widna hae been sae bad if it had been a lady's bicycle with the parallel bars in the frame, bit it wis an aul' wifie's bike that I got, an' I wisna a' that pleased. My father, wi' scant regard for my feelin's, simply pintet oot that a wifie's bike wis better than nae bike ava. Tae detract fae the ignominy o' the aul' wife's bike I decided that I wid mak' a propellor an' it wid be nae ordinary propellor at that. There wis nae timmer thrown oot in my father's day. Onything that cam' intae the category o' a 'gweed board' was reverently set aside for future use. The rest was hackit up for kindlers. I fell in wi' a bit that fitted neither group; it was ower gweed for kindlin' bit ower short tae be classified as a board. I hid tae wyte until my father was oot on a hire so that I could tak' a shot o' his spokeshave. I ruggit an' tuggit at the fower edges o' the bit stick until I hid the leadin' an' trailin' edges chamfered tae my satisfaction, bored a hole in the middle an' nailed the blade on tae a blockie o' wid. A lick o' paint an' the thing wis ready tae mount on the bike. I'd gi'en it three colours, reid, fite and blue, tae mak' it look like an RAF bomber fan it furled. It must ha'e been fairly well balanced for it began tae spin afore I got up the close. I headed for the village to show my pals fit I'd made. I gathered speed and leaned ower the guys o' my bike tae see the full effect o' this thing o' beauty that I hid created. Noo the A96 then wisna like the A96 noo. Ye only saw a car noo and again. In other words, traffic didna come intae the equation at a'. But this must ha'e been a Setterday for that was the day that Alsop the butcher's van cam' roon' an' it wis parkit at Jimmy Cryle's front gate. I wid ha'e miss't the van—I'm sure eneuch o' that; it wis something else that got in my road. Aul' Hendry, the bobby fae Pitcaple, wis up in the village that day and he hid jist stoppit for a news wi' Jimmy and the butcher. He wis leanin' on his bike, oot by the tail o' the van, near half ower the road when suddenly he was attacked by a low-flying RAF bomber cunningly disguised as a wee loon on an aul' wifie's bike. The next I kent I wis lyin' in the ditch at the ither side o' the road. The full horror of what I'd done dawned on me when I saw the bobby's uniform. I wis up and on my bike so fest that hid it been forty years later I'd hae gotten the Norman Tebbit Gold Medal. I can hear Jimmy Cryle lauchin' yet as he cried oot, "Ha ha Donal' ye've fairly hit the wrang lad this time." My pedal had gaen intae the hin' wheel o' the bobby's bike, buckled it and broken some spokes. When my father cam hame fae his hire he had the bobby's bike tae sort. I often winnert fit wye I hidna gotten a hidin' but my mither tellt me later that aul' Hendry hid been adamant, "Noo Jimmy, nae need tae tak' it oon on the loon for he got a big eneuch fleg as it wis!"

I had various cast-off bikes fae then until I left the skweel at fifteen. In atween leavin' and startin' my apprenticeship, I made the price o' a brand new, beatin' grouse up in Lumsden. I chose a Raleigh Lenton Sports and we did thoosands o' miles the'gether. I bikit oot and in tae my work in Aiberdeen in the fine days. I wid race Alexanders bus hame as far as the Oyne Fork which prompted Charlie Gordon to suggest to me that I wis surely the festest chiel in Aiberdeenshire on a push-bike. But Charlie wis wrang. I took tae gaun tae the various Sports if there wis bike races at them and though I could beat maist o' them I never got the better o' Davie Gill. He had a Raleigh Super Lenton and, man, he could mak' it shift. Nae matter fit sports I gaed tae, Davie wis there; he wis first and I wis second. I bikit oot tae Aboyne ae Friday night so that I could ha'e a go at the bike races at Tarland Sports on the Setterday. There wis three races, the quarter mile, half mile and the mile. There wis some gey hardy lookin' lads there but tae my great delight there wis nae sign o' Davie Gill. Maist o' the ither lads hid helpers wi' them so that they could be mounted on their machines, feet in their tae straps ready for aff when the gun wis fired. I kent fine that the helpers werena' haudin their men back either. I had nae sic luxury and fan the signal cam' I had tae throw my leg ower, furl my pedal and try tae get my fit intae its cage. By this time I hid lost a fair bit o' grun and in the short quarter mile three lads had crossed the line aheed o' me. I had mair time tae catch up in the half mile and cam' in second, gainin' on the winner a' the time. I just kent the mile wis mine for the takin' and after a hale season o' frustration, the announcer sayin' my name wis gaun tae be music in my ears. There wis simply a question o' by fu much.

Weel, a shoo'er o' rain cam' on so I gaed intae the competitors' tent and there I met in wi' an affa fine mannie, McKenzie the dancer. He had jist nae lang cam' hame fae Sooth Africa faur he hid haen a gran' time and he wis lettin' me see some photographs fae there. We were gettin' on like a hoose on fire and I jist happen't tae look oot o' the door o' the tent. There wis the bikers takin' roon' the park in the mile race. I'd been that busy newsin' I'd miss't the announcement. Tae croon it a', it poor't a' the wye hame fae Tarland.

My bikin' days were by fan my time wis oot. I sell't the Raleigh and aff I gaed tae dae my National Service. That brings tae min' my next heroic failure. Efter six weeks o' basic trainin' a'body got their postin's. Opposite my name wis Bordon P.L.A. I kent fine faur Bordon wis but I had nae idea fit PLA meant so I gaed and spier't at some o' the heid billies. I was tell't it stood for Potential Leading Artisan and that it wis considered a plum postin'. Noo then, Mrs McArthur, fit div ye mak' o' that?

So there I landed in Bordon on a forty-fower week course at the end o' which I wis tae be a sergeant. Nae sma' drink! The course was in twa pairts, the first twelve weeks wis a' aboot wir trade wi' exams at the end o't. Syne we hid tae be interviewed by the C.O., an' efter that a further thirty-two weeks wi' emphasis on the sodgerin' bit. At the start o't we were a' issued wi tool kits for the practical side o' oor trainin' an' ilka Friday nightwe hid tae pit them back tae the tool store. A'e Monday mornin' somebody came intae the classroom needin' me tae gang an' see the heid storeman chiel, a mannie wi' a croon on his sleeve. He proceeded tae tell me that my tools hid been stolen ower the week-end and that seein' they were signed for by me, I wad hae tae pey for them. I didna think it wis very fair, and said so, bit he pintit oot that rules were rules and regulations were regulations and there wis naethin' that he could dae aboot it. Bit he said it wad be time eneuch tae sort it oot at the end o' the twelve weeks. Noo I hid an aul'er brither an' he hid been an officer in his National Service days, so I drappit him a note sayin' that I didna think muckle o' Army rules and regulations and tell't him fit wye. He wrote back tae me and said he thocht they were bluffin', and at the end o' the course, if they persisted in calkin' me up for the tools, jist tae say that I wintit a Court o' Enquiry. That, apparently, they couldna refuse.

So there I wis facin' the mannie wi' the croon on his sleeve and he went on aboot fu they hid tried this and tried that but they'd nivver gotten the thieves nor the tools and fit a peety it wis bit I wad jist hae tae pey up. "Weel", said I, "I'm nae that happy aboot it and I wint a Court o' Enquiry intae the metter." Noo that kinda surprised the mannie wi' the croon on his sleeve and I wis despatched tae see a mannie wi' a croon on his shooder. This was Major Fletcher, officer-in-charge o' the workshops. He slivvered an' spat an' bristled and demanded tae ken fit a' this nonsense wis aboot so I jist explained tae him that my tools had been stolen while in the Army's toolstore faur I hid pitten them as I'd been tell't tae dae an' that the Army had lost them and they wintit me tae pey for them. I didna think it was a'th'gither richt hence my request for a Court o' Enquiry. That wid hae involved the C.O., bit as naebody had nivver tell't him aboot it in the first place, the tools were conveniently forgotten. I had won my battle bit the war wisna ower yet. Na fegs, I still hid tae get the C.O.'s recommendation tae get on tae the main pairt o' the course. Noo, I'd met the C.O. aince or twice and he seemed a fine kin' o' a mannie, bit dammit a'body needs a break and the C.O. gaed on leave. Weel, fa div ee think wis actin' C.O. when I gaed up for my interview? That's him, the mannie wi' the croon on his shooder. "Not suitable material", the report said. I had daen weel in baith exams and the Technical Adjutant said he couldna understand it, bit Mrs McArthur an' me, we kent fine.

She's been sittin' there on my shooder for half a century, my secret Nemesis, in black frock and coat. I've pit it a' doon on paper in a vain attempt tae exorcise her ghost. I jist hope there wis nae significance in that dream I had the ither nicht. I wis rinnin' up the Kirkgate, envelope in hand, and there she was at the Bookshop door shakin' her heid, an' sayin', "Na na Laddie, ye're ower late."

DONALD PENNY

Blow the Man Down

Luckily for the citizens of Aberdeen, Rory Woollard was incapable of putting the key into the door of his Porsche. He'd been working on the theory that if he could get the door open he was fit to drive. A cold fist of air snatched the lie from his open mouth. He reeled backwards. Wine, bottled beer, brandy and liqueurs slammed a message through his bloodstream; he'd better get a taxi. The Big Man had laughed at one of his jokes; he'd seen the twitch of the Big Man's eyelid when promotions were being talked of; he'd heard his name whispered openly over canapés. He'd left early, "work to do in the morning". It was no time to blot his copybook. Blowing a kiss to the tall glass building and neon Oil Company logo, he staggered out of the parking space.

In the cosiness of the function suite he'd been sweating comfortably. Outside, the cold gripped him and plastered his shirt to his chest. His jumper was in the car. Leaving shelter made him gasp. He bumped into a huddled figure in a heavy coat, turning into the opening with downcast eyes.

"Where d'you think you're going!" demanded Rory.

There was no reply. The man tried to sidestep, to reach a corner away from the wind. He had a grimy kitbag on his shoulder. His pate was bald, red from the abrasive weather.

"Oh no you don't. This isn't a public thoroughfare. Find a cardboard box to sleep in!" Rory collared the man and shoved him off in the other direction.

"Riff raff," he muttered, "drunken trash."

He flagged a taxi. But he had to stop the car half way through the ride. Its acceleration force was too much for his stomach. He couldn't risk making a mess of the back seat.

"Let me out," he choked, waving a five pound note.

"Here?"

"Anywhere, fool . . . can't breathe . . . augh . . ."

He made it just in time, threw up in one big throw, turned around to see if the taxi was still there. The tail lights were far away. He was stranded. "Blast those prawn vol-au-vents!" He straightened up and opened his eyes wide. He was back in the strong wind; this time being funnelled down a narrow cobbled alley. He backed into a recess, dim and shadowy and smelling of damp. A polythene wrapper whipped up from the cobbles. He raised an arm to fend it off. It halted a moment in mid air and rose like a kicking swimmer high toward the tops of the derelict buildings hemming him in. Tenements—no, warehouses; boarded windows, dry rot fug, soiled brick, rusted wire mesh. Even the litter looked antiquated and neglected.

"Nobody from the Company ever uses that taxi firm again," he promised the bricks.

He had an idea of where he had been dropped, and felt insulted on principle. A clogged rhone threw down gobs of yesterday's rain. He dodged the windthrown sparks. He tramped in his own mess . . . injury added to insult. He made for the lamplight at the end of the alley.

The vista that opened up was one even postcards couldn't romanticise.

Behind a curtain of mesh stolid vessels nudged the harbour rim. There was no water to be seen; only the feel and smell of it. The wind hit him smack! like the belt of a bitter bride. He blew backwards, anchoring himself to a lamp post. Sensing a lull he cast himself onto the pavement and ran for shelter. A hasty look at his Rolex told him he had time before the harbour pubs shut shop. Time enough to warm himself and call a taxi.

He charged into the nearest pub. The warmth was wonderful, the beer and tobacco smell cosy and alluring. A jukebox played, and an aroma of toasting cheese made his stomach temporarily forget its bruises. It would have been the perfect pub, he thought, if it wasn't for the seedy clientele. But he'd suffer them. Anything was better than to be outside with neither coat nor jumper. If anyone here wanted trouble, he'd handle it. He'd had kung fu lessons; he'd been out for the school rugby team.

The place was traditional: that is to say, its budget didn't run to parquet flooring, hessian walls, glass doors, chrome tubing, spot lamps or art noveau prints. In places the plastic floor covering was worn through to the stone, one big ashtray. Warmth was supplied by body heat and a pair of mismatched radiators.

Rory expected immediately to be the centre of attention, but he wasn't. The rush for drinks before the bell made coatless strangers a low priority. With exaggerated haughtiness he made room at the bar. A hunched black figure on a barstool glared hatred at him, more from habit than conviction. Quizzically, the barmaid served him a gin and forgot him.

At a table in the middle of the pub, next to a single square pillar, sat an elderly, thin-boned man and a young girl. They would have been of no consequence to Rory if they hadn't included in their sphere of influence the only free seat in the sparsely furnished space. He went through the necessary formality—"This anyone's?"—got a grudging nod from the girl, scraped the chairlegs far back from his companions.

The old man made him feel uncomfortable. He was bolt upright in his chair. Narrow, sunken eyes embedded in a web of cracks and wrinkles were so expressionless as to make the man seem blind. Yet, no matter how Rory leaned and shifted, the black eyes were always on him.

Rory turned his attention to the girl. He was too drunk to be discreet about it. He peered at her like she was a video display. She coloured and looked away.

She was pretty, no more than twenty years old. Her hair was rich red, naturally curled, her skin pale but warm. She too was underdressed. Through a baggy cotton top he caught the contours of a well filled brassiere. The top was wide necked. It revealed her throat, part of her shoulder, the flat smooth space above her cleavage. She had good skin. Canvas trousers, baggy everywhere but at her hips, obscured the shape of her legs. But when she crossed her legs the coarse material tightened to her backside and Rory could tell she was well porportioned. His first thought was "What's a nice girl like this—?" Then he snorted audibly. Nice girl my foot!

He examined her profile. She had a button nose and slightly protruding lower lip. He found her girlish cuteness appealing. There were things he would never pay for . . . Still, he couldn't help wondering how much? Pimply Ron in accounts could no doubt have told him.

He toyed with the idea. The grossness of the idea struck him and made him laugh aloud. The girl noticed. Turning full on she gave him a look full of blank challenge. At the same time the wind rattled the windows violently enough to make Rory jump.

It was his turn to colour. He fidgeted and patted his jacket for cigarettes. He came up with an empty packet.

"Hae ane o' these."

Without taking her eyes off him, the girl had lifted two cigarettes from an open packet next to the old man's whisky glass. She offered one across the table. Rory hesitated before accepting it. He gave her a light from his gold Ronson.

"I ken what you're thinkin'," the girl said, keeping up eye contact. "Hae a lookie ower there though."

He followed the direction of her cigarette and saw the wording on a sign over the bar—NO HOOKERS, NO CREDIT, NO CHEQUES, NO DRUNKS—MEAN NO POLIS! quipped the stencilled board. He couldn't escape the firmness of her blue-green eyes. He thought she was angry. But her Aberdeen lilt was even and low, almost intimate.

"Just tellin' ye what the score is," she said, sitting back. The old man was trying to extricate a cigarette for himself, without lifting the packet. His trembling fingers were unequal to the task. The girl left him to it. Rory found the old man's clumsiness unbearable to watch. He reached across to help. The trembling fingers clenched to a fist and slapped down protectively on the packet.

"Never mind Uncle Jockie. He's like that efter whisky. He shouldna' smoke anyway. He's nae supposed tae, wi' his heart."

"Is there time for another drink?" slurred Rory, looking at her shoulder and deciding the old man was best ignored.

She shrugged. "Closin' time changes every night doon here. Nae-body's shouted yet."

He offered to buy her a drink. She accepted with no great enthusiasm. He opened his wallet, displayed some plastic, carefully skimmed a note from a neglected wad. He was gratified to note a new glimmer of interest.

"Is there a phone here?"

"Used tae be. It got broken."

He asked to use the phone behind the bar. There wasn't one. The phone was upstairs in the landlord's flat. "He's away, the door's locked, sorry darlin'." He would have to flag another cab.

Or go home with the red haired girl! It wasn't an impossibility. She was OK. And he was good looking, well off. She'd think him quite a catch, surely.

"What do you do for a living?" he asked her, after a dull clinking of glasses.

"This and that. There's nae much goin'. I fancy bar work, but the students have got a' them, now that there's nae much proper pubs left—just wine bars and cafe bars and a' that stuff." Her nose crinkled.

Her name was Estelle. She's been married for a year after school, then she'd "wised up". She had a flat "roond aboot here", and spent most of her time in the dole, in the pub, or working part time when she could get it. She had a boyfriend now and then, but they were "a' a bunch o' wasters." She was "practically a virgin," she told him. Uncle Jockie was no relation. She just knew him.

Before long they were sitting elbow to elbow; she leaning into him, the top folding out to allow him an interesting vista, making up for his boredom with her conversation. The old man appeared to be asleep in his chair, or catatonic.

Roy fancied his chances more and more. He bragged, postured, namedropped, quoted salaries—even gave her a rundown on the last service bill for the Porsche. He was having strange thoughts.

Hilary, his partner, had walked out on him, exasperated, weeks ago. It meant he had been short of a consort at tonight's function. Gin had blunted his contempt for Estelle. With the right dress, the right jewelry, the right make-up, she'd be more than a match for skinny Hilary with her mannish, politically aware eyebrows and sharp knees. Provided she could learn to keep her gob shut—but that was a problem with all women.

Someone was eavesdropping. When Rory mentioned where he lived, a harsh male voice rasped behind him: "aye, youse oil fowk like tae keep tae yer ain bittie, right enough. Like ye were affronted tae bide in the toon that feeds ye!"

It was the man who had scowled at Rory from the barstool, still doing up his fly on the way back from the toilet. A long look, undecipherable, passed between him and the girl. It ended with his grinning horribly.

"Mind your ain business, Markie." She suddenly rose and donned her jacket. "Come on, let's get oot o' here. I'll show ye the best way tae get a taxi."

She waited impatiently while Rory finished his drink. The black figure hunched back down in its stool.

"Who was he?" Rory shouted, against the gale assaulting the open door. She gave him no answer. She led him out. They walked a few yards and rounded a corner.

"Ower there. Ye'll get a taxi that isna just lookin' for hookers and their men." She pointed to the top of the alley, towards the carriageway. She turned on her heels. He grabbed her before she could go. He had projected his desires too far forward to let her leave now. His ideas were wild . . . She owed him something just for his fancying her . . . He was at least due a kiss . . . She didn't take him here just to give directions . . .

He tried to put his hand inside her jacket. The wind helped him, whipping the material conveniently aside. It rattled in his ears. He could hardly hear his own thoughts, let alone her protests.

"Leave!" cried Estelle.

He grabbed her tighter, pushing his head close to hers. She struggled.

"Leave her be—NOW!" commanded another voice.

It was Markie; fists clenched, feet apart, scowling aggressively. Rory leapt back. Estelle did up her jacket.

"He winna pay," came her expressionless voice.

Markie advanced. He grabbed Rory by the lapels. Rory was taller, but the strength of the grip made him wary. He tried to kick, to move away. It was impossible.

"He winna pay," Estelle repeated.

Markie slammed him against the wall. A clawlike hand found his inside pocket. Let loose, all he could do was give himself up to the support of the cold bricks. The black coated figure browsed the inside of his wallet.

"Thirty quid. Cheap at the price."

"We did nothing!" Rory protested. "We'd no time. This is plain robbery, you—"

The palm of Markie's hand struck him into silence.

The old man hobbled on to the scene. Estelle moved to his side like a coy schoolgirl.

"Pit anither ten poun' on it," he croaked. "He'd a half hour o' her time in there . . . Aye, an' a fag o' mine tae top it!" He watched with hooded eyelids while the wallet was divested of the extra charge. The wallet was tossed at Rory's feet. By the time he'd picked it up all three were gone, leaving him humiliated and exhausted, disgusted by his own stupidity.

The wind blasted up the alley. It knocked him sideways. His hand made moist contact with something messy. That was the last straw. He drew a couple of deep breaths. He straightened out his mind. They weren't going to get away with this. He made his way back to the pub.

They weren't there. Undaunted he stalked the harbour wall.

The vessels in their berths were barely lit. The backdrop of colourless half lit sky made the funnels and masts and derricks appear insectlike, menacing. Music scraped and whistled through the wires. A few drunks were struggling home, shift workers leaned forward in the blow, letting it blast away the heat of their labours. A kerb crawler cruised abreast of him for a full minute, wheels rumbling on the cobbles.

The street was coming alive as the pubs emptied. He pushed on, up and down, searching backstreets and alleys. He looked wild, he was so singleminded in purpose. He became unaware of time, or of the icy wind that had somehow become his element. He stared and was stared at. Strangers stepped off the pavement to let him by.

At last, many yards ahead of him, he spotted a short, heavy coated man scurrying at speed. He ran after the familiar back. For a while he thought he was running on a treadmill—that the gap between he and his quarry would never lessen. Unbridled hatred kept him going. Gasping with cold and exertion he finally caught up.

When he was close enough to grasp a shoulder his mind was only on one thing.

He threw the man to the ground, smashed his fist into the side of his head. Hands went up to protect the face. Rory kneeled on him with all his weight, pummeling till he was exhausted. He patted the man's coat and came up with a dog-eared wallet. He counted out four bills.

Before he could pocket them he felt his weight rise off the ground. He was in restraint, his legs blowing like rags in the wind. He resisted. But the last of his energy was gone.

"Enough o' that, son. Do it quietly. It'll go better with you in the long run."

The policeman looked kindly but determined.

Rory all but sighed with relief. The police! He could explain to them, have everyone put in jail. A policeman was helping the man up. He would try to run. "Then they'll know," thought Rory, "then they'll see who's the criminal."

But though the man was familiar, the bloodied face wasn't Markie's.

Rory gaped. The man gesticulated crazily, howling his indignation in a foreign accent. "I look only for a place to sleep! Nobody let me sleep! I miss boat—get into mission tomorrow maybe! I have bad time! He jump on me, he hit me, he take money—!"

The words escaped Rory; he was taken up with the shining bald pate, the heavy coat, the soiled kit bag he had failed to notice in his pursuit . . .

"Please—it's all a mistake. I'm sorry, really—"

It was no good. He had muck on one hand, blood on the other, dried sick on his shirt, mud on his shoes, his jacket was torn, and his hair, loaded with gel at the start of the evening, stuck up in an alarming quiff. He was typical late night street litter.

The Big Man of course heard about the incident.

A few weeks later, Rory Woollard was boasting about being the best dressed client at the Job Centre.

PETER D McMILLAN

Wullie's UFO

It wis the day afore the village fête,
We waur a' yokkit doon on The Green,
Settin up stalls and the big Marquee
Fin yellin' disrupted the scene.
Big Wullie Tamson, reed-faced an gaspin'
Hurtled doon thro' the lane on his bike,
"Ye'll nivver believe fit I've jist seen,
Man, I've nivver afore kint the like.
A UFO—stop shakkin' yer heid,
Am tellin' the truth, or God strike me deid.
A big fite blob is a' I can say,
Bit there it wis as plain as day.
It haivered a file for a' tae see
Tho' naebody else did—jist me.
I dinnae ken fit to make o' it,
It's beyon' ma understandin',
An' afore ye ask, I'd ma glaisses on,
'Cause I wis undercoatin' the landin'."
"Weel, pit yer glaisses on noo" we said,
"Ye micht as weel help fin yer here,
If ye hing yon posters an' plant thae signs,
Ye'll be first in line for a beer."
So, grabbin' a bundle o' posters,
Wullie took his specs frae their case,
As he pit them on—it began tae dawn,
Ye should o' seen his face.
For his UFO wis noo on show
A' fite an' shiny bricht,
Nae mystery craft,
"Man, Wullie yer daft—
It's pinnt on the lens on the richt."

MAUREEN LEETE

Moving On

She moved on Sunday—
They weren't religious.
And on Monday my mother said
There was something on the door of the cottage,
So we went over.

It was only chipped paint
Making a mark on the door like paper.

Then with morbid curiosity
We skirted the cottage
And peered through the threadbare glass:
A few boxes,
Old lightbulbs,
A chest of drawers.

Remnants only,
Poor reminders,
No longer serving any useful purpose.

I lead the way through the gate
Into the old garden,
The drystone walls
And the path down the middle
And the flowers in front of the house.

She'll miss her flowers, mother said,
The wallflowers are just out,
She was a good neighbour.

And we came away
Up the road
Far apart as we walked,
And thought our own thoughts
And treasured our own memories.

SUSAN LUMSDEN

Goodbye and Hello

"I don't want to," I said, but it was no use. Aunt Aggie took me firmly by the hand and led me into the sitting-room where my father was lying in his coffin. I had no desire to see him dead; I think I had a subconscious fear that there would be on him some horrible sign of the massive, sudden, once-only heart attack that had killed him at his desk. As we reached the coffin, she let go of my hand. I remember noticing the dents in the carpet made by the trestles and wondering —stupidly—if my mother would be annoyed. Funny to think of that—a practical question overlaying the facts of death and sorrow.

Aunt Aggie bent over the coffin, stroked my father's forehead, and, to my horror, kissed his cheek. "Goodbye laddie," she whispered, and stood back, indicating that I should approach. Unwillingly I dragged my feet towards the coffin and stood looking down. My father's face was calm and stern, as in many of his photographs, hiding his natural kindliness, but my father was not there. I realised for the first time the truth of what I had read, that the body is simply an envelope for the soul. I couldn't speak or touch him. My aunt did not try to persuade me. We left the room and thankfully I went to the kitchen to put on the kettle, for the fifth or maybe the sixth time that day. Making tea was a comforting punctuation of the dragging hours.

There was no-one else in the house; my mother had taken the dog out for a walk and my sister had not yet arrived from London where she worked. For the first time in my life I was alone with Aunt Aggie. I knew that she was my father's oldest sister—twelve years older in fact—and that she had brought him up after his parents had died of tuberculosis within a few months of each other when he was about five, but that was all I knew. I didn't see her very often—we lived about fifty miles apart—no distance at all nowadays, but in the 1930s and 1940s, as we didn't have a car, it could have been two hundred. Also, six years of my growing-up had taken place during the Second World War, when you didn't get on a train or a bus unless there was a good reason—and a visit to a relative wasn't very often reason enough. At the time of my father's death my aunt would have been sixty-six, not a great age in fact, although I at nineteen, thought of her as old. She had always seemed to me to be a brisk, no-nonsense sort of person, sparing of speech, of whom I was, not afraid, but shy. But here she was, sitting slumped at the kichen table, her hand shielding her eyes, shaken with a deep, deep sigh. When I put the tea down in front of her, she rubbed her hand over her eyes and picked up the cup, curling both hands round it. It was the month of May and quite warm, but I knew that she felt cold, as I had, ever since hearing of my father's completely unexpected death.

"He wis my bairn," she said, and I knew what she meant. To all intents and purposes she had been his mother. "Mair nor the ithers," she went on. "Even Jimmie, he wis jist siven fin faither died, but he niver seemed tae mean the same. Ach!" she suddenly cried out, almost fiercely, "I should 'a died afore him!" I was shocked by the unexpectedness of her cry, but her naked emotion touched me deeply and I was suddenly seized with a desire to know more about my father as a child, before anyone else arrived and I was once more parlaysed with the shyness that had always been the greatest burden to me.

"What was he like when he was wee?" I said. "Why was he so special to you?" Ordinarily I would not have asked such a question, but it had been such a strange day altogether, and I felt almost lifted out of my usual self. "He wis a good wee loon maistly," she said. "Mind you, he could be ill-tricket as weel. Once he put a frog in my bed, and I got sic a fricht I let the pig fa' and the water went a' ower the fleer. I wis gain' tae gie him a richt lickin', but he lookit at me wi' sic a mischievious look on his face I jist hid tae lauch!" She drank some more of her tea and then said, "Mind you, for a wee thing he wis real sensitive. He aye seemed tae ken if I hid a sair heed or wis feelin' doon." Her eyes were filled with tears now and I thought that she might not go on, but she cleared her throat and went on, "He wis aye fond o' readin' from his first days at the school. I mind the infant mistress tellin' me that he 'devoured his reading book as if it was nourishment'. I thocht at the time it wis a fancy kin' o' thing tae say, but I could see it wis like that later masel'. She aye keepit up an interest in him, Miss Cordiner, and lent him books oot o' her ain shelves. There wis nae money at hame tae buy onything like that." I had a sudden vivid picture of my father, sitting in the chair that had been pushed back to make room for the coffin, lost to the world, deaf to conversation and questions addressed to him. The fire could have died completely on a winter's evening and he would have been oblivious to the cold. "What else did he like doing?" I asked, wondering if he'd had some talent that had been allowed to wither, for I had never seen him pursue any other hobby at home. "He likit the Scottish dancin'," said Aunt Aggie. "Ane o' the teachers at the school wis affa interestit, and she got some o' the loons tae jine in. Charlie niver minded his brithers ca'in him a saftie." I could see that determined little boy, facing his brothers' ridicule with equanimity and a rare maturity. I knew that my father had won medals in the army for Highland Dancing, but I hadn't realised how early his interest had begun. Another scene flashed into my mind, of my sister and me, collapsing with laughter as Dad roared in mock fury at our grossly inept young efforts at the Highland Fling and the Sword Dance. I felt the sting of the first tears since I'd been told of his death. I was recognising the man I knew in the picture my aunt was painting of the child I had not known.

"And later?" I said. "What did he want to be?" I knew that he had given a false age to get into the army, being only sixteen at the outbreak of the First World War, and had remained in the army all his life. But had he really wanted to be a soldier? Aunt Aggie's answer was a surprise. "He wid hae likit tae ging tae the University and be a doctor, but there wis nae money for that, and he kent. He didna tell me that's fit he wid 'a likit till efter he came hame in 1918." I wondered if that unsatisfied desire had gnawed at him through his years in military service. I had thought him perfectly content with his lot, but what do young people, immersed as they are in their own selfish growing-up, know of what is in their parents' hearts?

"How did you manage for money?" I asked—another question that normally I would never have presumed to put. "Did you have a job?" Aunt Aggie gave a little laugh. "We lived in a cottage four miles oot o' Torphins, and there wis nae wey I could get tae the toon tae work. "I helpit at the hairst an' the tattie pickin', bit I hid tae be there for the bairns fan they cam' hame frae the school, or they'd hae been taen awa' fae me and I couldna' hae that. I kent my mither wid hae winted us tae bide thegither." She sipped her tea reflectively and I held my breath, afraid that she wouldn't continue. She had already spoken more in the last quarter of an hour than during all the visits over the years. Perhaps she found it a relief to speak of her dearly loved child to someone who had also loved him. However, she continued, "It wis aye difficult, but we managed. We got a little fae the Police Welfare Fund, an' the aulest twa were workin'—yer Aunti Annie at Fyvie Castle, she wis a maid, and Alec wis fee'd at the Meldrums' fairm. He aften brocht hame a bag o' tatties, and a neep or twa, and Geordie at the mill used tae gie's a pucklie oatmeal. But shoes—they were jist for the winter, and I wis a dab han' at makin' doon the aulest anes' claes for the little anes. I'd been used tae lookin' efter things for a whilie; my mither hid been real nae weel for two three years afore she died." There was no self-pity or bitterness in her voice; she had just done what had to be done.

"Did you never feel that you just couldn't manage?" I said, fascinated by this glimpse of a life I had never had to endure, and appalled to realise that when she had taken on this burden, my aunt was only eighteen, a year younger than I was then, I who had never had to take responsibility even for myself. Aunt Aggie gave a small laugh. "Mony's the time," she said. "But I jist said a prayer and the Lord aye provided." She spoke quite unselfconsciously, as if talking of a friend. "I mind aye time, though," she went on, "I'd seen the bairns awa' tae the school and I sat doon at the table and hid a good greet, because there wis naethin' in the hoose for their denner, nae even a tattie. I didna ken fit I wid dae, but I micht hae kent that the Lord wid be lookin' efter us, because young Alickie Donald come tae the door an' said his mither hid the bile and could I come up tae the fairm and work tae her, and nae tae worry aboot the bairns' denner, there wis enough broth in the pot for a'body. I niver remember it sae bad again. And fin I wis twenty-three I met yer Uncle Bob, and he aye helpit us oot, even afore we got mairrit."

I gazed at my aunt. "I could never have done what you did," I said. "You niver ken fit ye can dae till ye're faced wi't," said Aunt Aggie.

Just then I heard the front door open and the scrabbling of the dog's paws in the passage. Aunt Aggie looked at me, knowing as I did that the time for intimacy was past. She stretched out her hand to cover mine briefly, and said, "Come and see me soon, and I'll tell you mair if you wint." "I will," I said, my throat tight and painful, and the tears beginning to roll down my cheeks. "I will." I felt that my grief in saying goodbye to my father, had been eased by saying hello to the child he had been.

EVA J COWIE

A Chance Encounter

Up amongst the towerin' crags,
I chanced tae meet a couple hags,
Wizened faces, legs sae thin,
Silver hair an' sunbaked skin.

Anoraks, tattered, torn,
Knitted toories, heads adorn,
Canvas gaiters, splattered, worn,
Feet, wi' boots aa battered shorn.

Hangin' loosely on their backs,
Sma' an' faded canvas packs,
Horn-topped walkin' sticks held tight,
They really looked an affa sight.

As I approached they sipped some tea,
An' each ane hid a glance at me,
I passed them by, gave each a nod
An' proudly up the path I trod.

I quickened pace, wi' zealous vigour,
I really looked an awesome figure,
Waterproofs, fluorescent red,
Make me seen for miles it's said.

Boots aa shiny wi' the rubbin',
Aa last week wi' heated dubbin,
In them ye can see yer face,
An' aince again I quicken pace.

Nylon gaiters, shinin', blue,
Cover socks, twa pairs, brand new,
Nylon mittens o' the best,
I set aff faster, wi' mair zest.

On mi back a rucksack blue,
Wi' coontless pockets, stormproof too,
In it lots o' extra gear,
Like first aid kit, an' tins o' beer.

Balaclava, some dry socks,
Cheese an' chocolate in a box,
Toilet paper, well ye ken,
It could be days before yer hame.

A torch, a whistle jist in case,
Ye fa' an' brak yer leg some place,
Then six lang blasts upon it toot,
An' hope there's ithers gaun aboot.

Roon mi neck a bit o' string,
Ye'll find a compass there dis hing,
An' on mi belt a plastic pocket,
Saves mi map fae gettin' soakit.

On the map wi journeys traced,
Worked oot afore this day I faced,
Wi' compass bearin's as I go,
I'll find mi wye in rain or snow.

Now ye can see why I'm sae proud,
I really staun oot in a crowd,
Nae winner thon twa wifies glanced,
The sight o' me hid them entranced.

But as along the track I stride,
There's jist one thing that dents mi' pride,
Wi' aa mi gear an' expert plannin',
Why do they pass an' leave me staunin'?

Now there's a moral tae my tale,
I winner if ye see it,
"It's nae sae much o' fit ye've got,
But fit ye can dae wi' it."

CHARLES HILTON

Pom

Our first Postman was 'Pom'. In a scattered country district a good postman is a valuable asset. He gets to know, from his daily round, when somebody needs care or attention. He normally delivers a newspaper and pays regular visits to elderly people living in small cottages on the hillside.

Such a man was 'Pom'. That, of course, was not his real name. He was known as 'Pom' because, as he walked the roads of the parish he used to sing quietly to himself 'Pom, Pom, Pom, Pom' in a somewhat tuneless tone. Pom's postal area included three distilleries and the distillery cottages. When the weather was bad (and it could sometimes be very bad), or at a time of special celebration such as New Year, 'Pom' was fortified for his round. Sometimes, not often, he overdid it and on one occasion, on a wild wintry day, he was feeling the effects of his 'fortifying'. When he had a few drams he felt hot and had the urge to discard some of his clothing. On this occasion he arrived at Cardow with nothing on but the post bag. Somebody took him in and arranged for his mail to be delivered, but nobody ever reported him!

ROBERT PRENTICE

Handicap

My faither wis a postie, his wife a servant lass
He wis Bertie, she wis Nellie, as befits the workin' class.
It wis fan they hid their bairnies that they took the chunce tae blaw
They'd a Rosaleen, a Honor, an I'm Veronica.
Oh fa could bide in a tenement, oh fa could thrive ata
Oh fa'd get by in Torry wi' the name Veronica?

Jist think on how it sounded fan raucous Missis Main
Yelled loudly frae the stair-heid, "Fa hit ye Muggie Jane?
Wis it Charlie Broon or Robbie or that wicked Jimmy Law?"
An greetin Muggie clipin, "No Ma . . . Veronica."

Hear Missis Main bawl coorsely, "Ye needna try tae hide.
Ye leave my Muggie Jane alane or I'll skelp yer wee backside.
My Muggie niver hit you first. I'm gaun tae tell yer Ma
An tell her fit I think o' her an' her Veronica."

At bedtimes windaes opened an' Mithers 'heids popped out.
"Hey Jessie fetch up Bella or I'll gie yer lugs a clout."
"Bed Willie". "Joe an' Junet take Rosie up an a'."
My mother just called, "Rosaleen where's Veronica?"

I wis made tae spik quite proper . . . Aiberdonian wis taboo.
It made my pals cry, "Hey there! We're nae playin' wi' you.
Ye winna ca' the ropes or stot a ba' agin' the wa'
Yer jist a bloomin scunner . . . Ging away Veronica."

Prim'ry school I didna fit wi' my posh uncommon name,
A butt for a' the bullies that play the bullies game.
They wid chase me an they'd thump me an tear my claes awa'.
That's fit ye get in Torry if yer name's Veronica.

I couldna hide at playtime wi' nae wey I could ging,
Some quines wid guard the lavvies an the rest aroon me sing,
"Oh fa spiks Torry-English an affa la-de-da?
Nae Betties, Pegs or Pollies . . . jist feel Veronica."

Still Central school wis better . . . a three year spell o' grace
I got the nick-name Ronnie . . . th' only loon's name in the place.
I never got my title frae the ither quines ata
Tho' the grade four war-time teachers still said 'Veronica'.

I wis kent the hale school ower as the bright spark in 1A
An abidy wid cry oot, "Ronnie sit wi us the day
We're nae in the mood for working an ye'll laff the time awa."
Oh then how I was happy I was named Veronica.

Bit happiness is fleetin' . . . I met a handsome bloke,
Ae nicht he took me hame wi him tae meet his workin' folk
"Fa's this ye've brocht," his Mother said, "A bonny lass but sma'.
I'st Effie, Liz, or Gludys?" . . . "No my name's Veronica."

Oh I lost that hansome laddie an ither lads the same.
Aye I've hin some affa troubles wi my far ower funcy name.
My nightmares wak me screamin . . . I'm feart tae sleep ata.
I dream I'm back in Torry an my name Veronica.

So tak heed if ye've quinies, please cry them Vi or Vee.
Dinna dee tae bairnies fit my folks did tae me.
An hae peety fan I'm eighty for ye'll hear my neebours craw,
"Dae ye see that dottled wifie there . . . That's auld Veronica."

VERONICA NICHOLSON

Sound Advice

Another source of revenue for the Village Hall fund was the income from a Certified Location for the Caravan Club. The only drawback here was the marshy nature of the site, which led the local doctor (reasoning that all caravanners would have to use the 'placie' sometime) to put a warning notice in the toilet. The notice read "In case of difficulty, please contact Dr. Anderson, Tel. Glenlivet 273 where a landrover with towball is available".

ANDY DUFF

'Doddie Milne's Day o' the Green'

On a Sunday 'twis Doddie's last prayer o' the nicht,
"Lord, please mak the morn be winn'y 'n' bricht.
It's whiles a sair chauve for the bairn, him 'n' me,
So we're maybe nae a' that You'd wint us t' be.
But if we're nae Godly, at least we'll be clean!"
For a Monday wis Doddie Milne's day o' the green.

Wi' the wash hoose fire set the evenin' afore
'n' aathing t' han' at the back o' the door,
The cun'les, the washin' boord, claes pegs 'n' rope,
The scrubbin' brush, bleach 'n' a bar o' white soap.
Six o'clock in the mornin', rubbin' sleep fae 'er een,
A match started Doddie Milne's day o' the green.

Now at 'at time o' mornin' maist fowk wid agree
A wash hoose in winter wis nae place t' be,
Bit, each cun'le flickert it's wee bit o' cheer
'n' the fire, sookin draughts, spead a glow 'oer the fleer,
While ootside, the poles, streetcher'd ropes in atween,
Stood waitin' on Doddie Milne's day o' the green.

Wi' a tub fae o' claes in caul' watter t' steep,
She gid up 'n' waukend 'er man oot 'is sleep
Syne made the porridge, spread rolls, masked the tea,
Hid 'er breakfast, washed dishes, she'd plinty t' dee,
For a' ither jobs that weemen's aye deen
Nott daein' on Doddie Milne's day o' the green.

Wi' the bairn aff t' school she gid back doon the stair
Wi' stockin's rolled doon 'n' dustcappit hair,
Ready t' start, wi' the door on the sneck,
Shuttin' oot newsy neebours, she'd nae time t' claik.
'Twis on wi' 'er apron 'n' aff wi' 'er sheen,
'Tnott wellies for Doddie Milne's day o' the green.

There wis buckets 'n' sheets 'n' collars 'n' socks,
Tablecloths, peenies 'n' bloomers 'n' frocks,
Lang drawers 'n' semmits, her man's good white shirt,
'n' aathing else showin' the least sign o' dirt.
A washin' 'twid tak 'er near a' foreneen.
Sma' pleasure wis Doddie Milne's day o' the green.

Fae products t' help 'er she'd plinty t' choose,
Like Oxydol, Clensel, Lux Flakes, Dolly Blues.
Bit though labels claimed "Removes dirt with ease",
Doddie kint she'd t' mix 'em wi' pure elbow grease.
Bit nae eese o' girnin' it hid t' be deen,
A ritual wis Doddie Milne's day o' the green.

Wi' the mungle uncovered she trailed the thing ben,
Wi' lobster reid airms wi' the stren'th o' maist men.
'n' wi' tubs t' fill up 'n' biler t' teem,
She wid seen disappear in a wash hoose o' steam,
Dichtin suds aff 'er han', syne sweat fae 'er een.
A trauchle wis Doddie Milne's day o' the green.

So a' mornin' she washed 'n' soakit 'n' rubbed
'n' biled 'n' ladled 'n' lather'd 'n' scrubbed;
Caad 'em a' through the mungle, 'n' hung 'em t' dry,
Transformin' a backie wi' colour forbye;
'n' tenement fowk lookin' doon on the scene
Kint fine it wis Doddie Milne's day o' the green.

For wi' greenies crammed ful fae palin's t' dyke
O' win' flappit claes, though each seemed alike,
Fas whites were the whitest wis nivver in doot,
In a hale street o' washin's, Doddie's stood oot;
Nae bonnier washin' in a' Aiberdeen,
There wis pride in Doddie Milne's day o' the green.

Now gin aifterneen wi' the last o' them dry,
She gither'd them in 'n' put aathing by,
Syne humphit twa baskets o' claes up the stair,
Leavin' wash hoose sloosht oot 'n' greenie poles bare.
A washin' day past, eence the ironin' wis deen
'n' so ended Doddie Milne's day o' the green.

Nooadays, Doddie's machines dee the work,
'n' she's mair time on Sunday's t' ging ti' the kirk
T' gie thanks for 'er blessin's she sees a' aroon'
'n' t' pray that the bloody things winna brak doon;
'n' though mungles 'n' bilers are nae langer seen,
She still ca's a Monday her day o' the green.

JIM BREMNER

Poachers Incorporated (1929)

It all began when the laird accepted an offer of a hundred pounds from a rich tobacco magnate for the privilege of fishing in the river. The locals were edged out of what they considered their rights to an occasional salmon or trout. Most of them grumbled and looked on it as yet another injustice to be borne, but not Jock, the youngest of the group; he didn't stop his fishing in spite of the dire penalties involved. Nor was he ever caught, although many a time,—ah, well now . . .

The rebellion began on the bridge as Jock and a few close cronies were looking soulfully at the forbidden waters. Rab, the retired sett-maker, was always the first to know when a salmon took up residence in one of the 'holes' in the river.

"Six beautiful clean fish are lying up there," he confided sadly to the gathering.

Davie looked at him, frowning. "Then it's not right!" he exclaimed, testily, "Not fair at all! Jock, you could get the fish out! Away and have a go! We'll watch for the baillies."

Old Rab's eyes gleamed as he placed a hand on the shoulder of the best fisher among them.

"That's a good idea, Jock," he urged. "Some of us'll stand guard on the bridge here and it would be a good thing to have somebody on the top of the ridge yonder at the end of the stretch."

Jock considered the proposition. He was not a kirk man, but he was hard-working and honest. The temptation was great however. He nodded decisively.

"I'll have a go!"

"Take your laddie with you," suggested Rab. "Willie can watch for signals from us while you get on with the fishing. We can all wave our bonnets if there's any likely trouble."

Getting the rod was no problem. Old Tam the joiner hid it in wooden shelving "for a house at the other side of the river", and hurled the lot down to the bridge over the guys and seat of his bike. The waders were in his bag of "tools".

Jock and Willie proceeded to the first hole where Rab had seen a salmon. Peesies whauped and performed their aerial acrobatics to distract intruders from their nesting grounds, and there was a flash of colour as a mallard scuttled squawking from the cover of the bank.

At the first bend, Jock assembled the rod, not without a slight tremor of excitement in the tying of his cast. As he waded out into mid-stream, Willie, who was eight, moved upstream to get a clearer view of the lookouts.

Fifteen minutes later a silvery 20 pounder was netted and wriggling on the bank. No signals had been given, although it's doubtful if they would have been received anyway—you see, Willie had found a waterhen's nest in the rushes with eggs that had to be touched, and there were the most colourful marsh fritillaries fluttering about that had to be watched, and the rarest of river backwaters full of bandies that had to be caught . . .

The salmon was carefully hidden in the reeds. A joyous thumbs up was given to the watchers, who returned the signal, remembering not to throw their bonnets in the air.

Fifty yards upstream was pool number two. This time the deep water was on Jock's side of the river. He had to come at it from above. He was well aware of the overhanging tree, so how he managed to tangle the minnow in its lower branches is a mystery. It meant an unexpected job for Willie, who had to spiel up the tree to dislodge the bait. With all the commotion you would have thought that the salmon might have been wary, but it was hooked on the first cast (or rather the second cast if you count the tree mishap!) Jock couldn't believe his luck.

That fish, however, tried everything in the book to get away. Jock played it with great expertise, giving it its head as it ran, holding its head up and drawing it as it rested between its frenzied dashes for freedom. By the time it lay on the bank he was sweating. Meanwhile, how were the lookouts doing? Well, the men of World War One vintage were on guard with all their old zeal, but Willie? Oh my!—there was an old nest higher up the tree that had to be looked into, and down at ground level there were rodden suckers just the right thickness for whistles. It would have been daft not to have cut off a couple for future use . . .

And so number two fish was laid to rest by the side of the first.

Some folk say third time lucky but it was not so for Jock. To reach the third lie, a long stretch of bouldery river had to be negotiated. Half an hour passed. Jock was getting anxious, and it didn't help his temper much when he turned round and found Willie flat on his back, testing various blades of grass between his thumbs to see which would produce the best skreich. His angry shout coincided with his foot landing on a slippery boulder and down he went. He got up just as quickly though for the water was wet—and it had got into one of his boots! Enough of that hole!

Jock came ashore.

Willie was trembling as his father emptied out the water from his wader. Luckily, the weather was warm and once the sock was wrung out it didn't feel so bad to wear. Jock's sporting instinct overcame his discomfort, and he decided to have one last go.

Willie now really was on guard—mind you, he was tempted to make a rush hat for himself, as the rushes were fine and long . . .

The next hole resembled the first,—a long shallow part with pebbles on the near side below. It was where kids (chaperoned of course) came to wade in summer. On his sixth cast Jock gave a shout of success; three fish in an hour and a half was not bad going. But going was the operative word, for Willie gave a shout too: the bonnets were in the air at the top of the furthest ridge!

But Jock would not let this one away, baillie or no baillie.

"Willie! In you go with the net," he cried. Willie hesitated.

"In you go man! Hurry! Boots and all!" he added. Willie was still hesitant.

"But Mum'll . . ." he began.

"I'll see to her," assured Jock. "Get in man. Never mind your clothes!"

Willie had never doubted his father's word. Boldly he waded in, net grasped firmly in both hands.

"Downstream of the fish laddie . . . Keep in the shallow . . . Careful now . . . I'll ease the fish over to you . . . Easy does it."

Willie was enjoying every moment of this adventure. He had been in the water fully clad before—when he failed to jump the burnie for a dare, down in the bogland. And a right good licking he had got for it! But this time the soaking was legal! And the fish was obliging. It was netted in no time and plunked in the rushes with the waders and rod—just in time! The watchers had vanished from the ridge and the laird and his dog appeared at a vantage point on the far beat. The laird's spyglasses raked the reaches of the river, but he saw only a man and his laddie walking towards him. The low power binoculars failed to reveal that the man was in his stocking soles and that the wee lad's boots were as heavy as lead and most uncomfortable. Finally, satisfied there were no poachers, the laird returned to his Ford and rumbled away. Jock's strategy had paid off.

As soon as darkness fell, the booty was retrieved with the same careful planning as before. Jock decided to hang the 12 pounder from his braces down the leg of his trousers with his huge army greatcoat hiding the bulge. Unfotunately however, he met the village bobby on the railway bridge. The friendly constable, always ready for a news, and knowing when to apply the law, kept Jock standing there as long as he could, thoroughly enjoying his awkward position in more ways than one.

Before the evening was out, Willie, carrying his precious oily Peter Lamp, was despatched to various houses in the unlit village with a basket. In it were slabs of salmon, wrapped individually in newspaper. These were for some of Jock's friends who were not so well off and who could keep their mouths shut.

This was just the first episode in Jock's long and successful career as a poacher: over the years the gang managed to relieve the tobacco man of many of his costly fish and in so doing kept themselves and their closest friends supplied with the food of the gods.

I can vouch for all this, for my name's Willie; and between the many plates of porridge I consumed as a boy I developed an insatable taste for poached salmon! Mmmmh! Nothing can beat it!

CHARLES W BROWN

Taking a Gamble

Another resident of the village, a lady retired from the faraway stock-broker belt, gave me a surprise when I was helping with the 1971 Census. In her eighties, she still had a very active mind, and I handed over the

Census form saying I would collect it in a week's time. Suddenly she called me back saying she was leaving for Reno Nevada the following morning. Having grown to expect anything of the glen folk I asked if she was contemplating a quickie divorce, but no, she said she was off "to play the tables", a hobby which she had already indulged twice, sailing to America on the *Queens*. This time, she said, she was flying KLM; and having gone with Postie Mackintosh's son to Dyce, would be over Glenlivet at around 4.30 p.m. the next day on her way to Amsterdam. She insisted I give her a wave—which I duly did!

ANDY DUFF

A Good Neighbour

Mrs Wills kept a few hens in her back garden, nice healthy creatures and very productive. I expect she thought of it as a nice paying hobby. One mother who had a surfeit of crusts in her bread bin at the end of the week filled a bag and gave them to her son to give to Mrs Wills for her hens. Unwisely, Mrs Wills, in return for the crusts, presented him with half a dozen eggs. Word got around and in no time Mrs Wills had innumerable callers with bags of crusts who were duly rewarded with eggs. Eventually Mrs Wills was seen buying eggs from the Co-op: I imagine she used some of them to hand out to her callers.

We soon heard that the hens had been sold; being the kind person she was, they could very well have been given away. I never knew whether Mrs Wills was unwise or just someone with a kind heart who couldn't turn her small callers away empty-handed.

DOROTHY GERRARD

A SENSE OF PLACE

Aberdeen Beach

a child runs
back and forth
through the waves   horizontally
                              between two sets of breakers
skeletal remains pulsed through vainly by saline solution
or simulated remains of beasts designed to take the sting
                                                out of the sea
he runs steadily not stopping
he is not going anywhere
he has arrived   he has caught the sun
                              harnessed the wind
                                    conquered

the waves which he reports in a brief rest
have thrown him a votive offering
a dead fish a salmon
he thinks   favoured child
                        acknowledged conqueror

but like all conquerors
he wants more he begins to run   vertically
                              not across but into
the sea
grabbing it in armfuls   I know
                              he cannot swim

further intelligence informs
it was not a salmon but a sea trout
that the sun and wind have escaped and the waves
                                    are making ground
it is time to retreat

                              II

a dead cormorant
we argued over the species but the forceful one
                        asserted its cormorancy

littering the beach
we tried to keep the dog away   what
did we expect   a distasteful scene
                                        of carnage
but the bird was dead
seasoned with specks of sand
lying in a dish designed
for a cormorant
                    the beauty of the sand
                                        shifing grave
dressed with beak and feet like
game in a boucherie

we need not have worried the dog knew this was
not dinner   but a lying in state
                                        we filed past
helpless
in the presence of the dead

it would be a gradual burial   no shovelling
of earth   hurried mutterings of benediction
and   the anxiety of the living to
                                        get the thing over

our cormorant would be effaced to the rhythm of
                                        the elements
gentle dispatch
a wake of wailing seabirds
bury me in sand   until I am stripped
                                        bones for the dogs
or mistaken for a wreck
become breaker for a while before
shifting   for I would prefer
                              not to stay in one place

would you be thought mad to want to count all
                              the grains of sand
the forceful one asked
contemplating a task for immortality
having to accept   that it was not a cormorant

III

a red boat pinned on the breast of the horizon
                        a sport for ever belonging to
a still red boat   which carries nothing
                    because it is two-dimensional
and going nowhere
                                    or waiting

ready or not here I come
a call from the beach hands wrenched from eyes
answered by nervous giggles
amongst the dunes

                                    the waves
                            aren't playing
they have their own game
what's the time Mr Wolf? with the shore
I am the shore I am Mr Wolf and I keep peeking
                ignore the noisy ones in the front
                you can always feel them coming
my eye is on
                            the last wave
                            at the back the
one that wears a brooch in the shape of a boat
a red one   will I be pleased to learn
                            it is my boat

a watched boat never comes   perhaps
but I think I will join the other game the one
                            in the dunes where
it is still possible to hide
                and to cheat
                            and I will not see
        the boat on the horizon start to move

IV

grey
pressed against the face of the town
                like a nylon face-mask
you   were a hand
the dog   a loop of leather

the children
                waited in a house besieged
the horizon   was a fire-curtain

beneath which more billows of grey
                        seeped through
                advanced in formation
            gravely rose for inspection

                        then lunged playfully
at fellow waves
already presented and
rebounding off the sea wall
                the fierce embrace sent
the knuckle-bones
clenched in my heart   flying
                    into the grey mist
                impossible to snatch back
    before the bounce of the next wave

what will I do without those knobbly
fears I cried abandoning the attempt

        but not wishing the mist to go
                    or the sea to calm
                            and leave
my scattered anxieties
easy pickings

                            V

a great crowd
                always a great crowd
    we descended running between
one single prone figure
and another
sphinxes
we open shapeless fidgety buzzing
between
silent forms of selfcontainedness
we cast grains of sand
even the dog   to the wind
            even the wind

amplified our immensity
blew out our hair our clothes our
voices   pneumatic figures
aside   those tightly tucked-in
          tucked-in faces
tucked-in thoughts
          we pushed them further
even though
     they could not go much further
     into the enigma of themselves

make yourself into a tiny ball be
as tiny as you can
          we could not be anything but
                              gigantic
like the desert
we seemed irreducible
                         but when
the grains of sand would not stay
          fell through my hands
                         I knew
what we could only know
               the terror of reduction
the secret of the sphinx
               was its irriducibility

then they rose in the evening sun
and we saw their tallness
gilded giants
departing

we scrambled onto shoulders
to form a pyramid
               made of sand
               it tumbled
     at the feet of the sphinx

VI

a narrowing band
in which to dodge dog-
     shit it's got me

our dog looks up
she is innocent
the band stretches
     tighter around the
     coast in the tension
I look back anxiously
          to the little one
armed with driftwood
guns swords lances
     but useless against
     the incoming tide
I am no Moses or
Neptune and they were
          not mesmerised
by twitching plastic
     temporarily beached
     gloves bags condoms
     nuzzled insistently
     by water suddenly
     inflating swimming
     off to join all the
other hand-like baggy
          phallic etc
     new-type fishes that
now colonise the deep
frog-marching the
little one we get to
the steps just as the
     band snaps and the
     waves hit the seawall

DEBORAH TRAYHURN

Boddam Questionnaire

Now if yi hail fae Boddam
or you're come o' Boddam stock,
Remember me ti a' ma freens
ti a' the Boddam folk.
Are the lichthoose beams aye piercin'
through the winter's rain an' sna?
Is the Skerry Rock aye lyin' aboot half a mile awa?

Div the bairns aye fish for podlies,
fin the summer's day is deen
Sine wander hame wi' stinkin claes betrayin' far they've been?
Div the waves aye pound wi' fury,
up the Big Cove an' the Sma'?
Are yon dods o' foam aye soarin' like I've never been awa'?
Are the folkies aye as kindly,
mindfu o' each ithers need?
Is there aye the cheery banter wi oor freens in Peterheed?
Div they ask "Fa hanged the monkey"?
an remind us o' oor past
Or has that ancient accusation been laid ti rest at last?
An' fit happens on a Sunday?
Is the brae aye black wi' folk,
ti hear wise admonition ti build upon the Rock?
For, min', the lichthoose an' the Skerry,
an, the Big Cove an' the Sma'
Through erosion or by ither means will some day pass awa.
An my freens that eence made Boddam the dearest place on earth
They were only passin' travellers wi' a common place o' birth.
Yet ever through these changing scenes,
stand One that's aye the same.
He once calmed stormy Gallilee, He healed the blind, the lame.
His constant call thro' a' the years,
is simply "Come to me."
Whit better antidote ti change than friendship close wi' He?

PETER CORDINER

Letter from Buchan—An Australian Writes Home

I wasn't looking forward to autumn. Suddenly it's icily damp and the days are declining rapidly into winter's dark. But this year an unusually lovely warm summer has slipped slowly into an exceptionally mild autumn with a higher than usual quota of dry, sunny days.

There are always some dry autumn days, not too windy, when it's pleasant to take the children on a picnic and collect rowan berries. Rowan trees—mountain ash—grow wild wherever they get the chance. There are plenty of these little trees in a wood nearby. The rowan is native to the north and west of Britain and although you see them elsewhere, to me they are an emblem of Scotland, just as the bright red berries are an emblem of autumn. Blue sky dotted with fleecy clouds; sun low all day, giving a golden light; pick, pick these tedious, bitter little berries that afterwards will be boiled, hung up in a muslin cloth to drip, and the juice boiled with sugar (one pound to one pint of liquid) until set into jelly. Eat it with lamb or mutton, or spread it on your bread if you like, though be warned—it's 'wersh' (Scots for 'sour'.)

Picking and bottling and preserving goes on at intervals from about July. Gooseberries, red and black currants, peas, beans, garlic and beetroot are all ready for us but there are still a few dregs of summer that could be put by for the cold days. If I can put up with the thorns I'll make some rosehip jelly the same way as the rowan, and this year there is even a sufficient crop of elderberries to tempt me to make some wine.

In these latitudes autumn used to be the season for all kinds of harvesting, and the rural communities were busy gathering in their winter provisions. (Oats, formerly the staple cereal, ripens later than barley or wheat.) Harvesting farm crops now affects only farmers, with the exception of potatoes. In the middle of October the children are off school for a week with their 'tattie' holidays. Once this was a vital means of ensuring that farmers had enough helpers to get in the potato harvest before the weather got really bad, because potatoes rot if they get frosted. It was a welcome chance for many families to earn money.

Up and down the country, fields would be full of gangs of people picking up the potatoes which the tractor-drawn lifter had unearthed. The potatoes are nowadays put into plastic washing baskets referrred to as 'skulls'. Women and children traditionally do this part, while the 'skullers', who are better paid and male, empty the full skulls into the trailer pulled by a second tractor. 'Picking tatties' is a back-breaking job because it can only be done by bending over from the waist and progressing stiff-legged up the row, hauling the skull along with one hand. Mechanical harvesters have replaced tatty squads in many places and a good thing too, you might think, but the job had its good side. Working in the open can be more enjoyable than working in a factory. For a start it's less noisy so there's more scope for banter and gossip, and there's a measurable beginning and end to the job so that when all the field is cleared there's some sense of achievement.

Another positive aspect of working outside is that you'll see many different birds, harbingers of the changing seasons. In autumn, little flocks of starlings start appearing on the electricity wires near our house, and the numbers grow as birds come in from Scandinavia. At dusk many flocks foregather over a Sitka Spruce plantation a few miles away, and their swooping and soaring goes on for a while until they all drop together on to their roosts in the trees.

The owners of pheasants have been late in letting out their birds this year. Carefully raised and tended in pens all these months, the pheasants now find themselves outcast, thousands wandering like refugees in fields, across roads, up tracks. I wonder how anyone manages to get such tame birds into the air to shoot at. There are also families of wild partridge about, their chicks well grown but not yet adult. One of the dogs frightened a hen partridge off her nest and we took the eggs home to set under a bantam hen, but the eggs were too small even for her, and broke.

Some miles to the east of us is the Loch of Strathberg, where huge numbers of geese from Scandinavia and Iceland overwinter. They congregate on the water at night and fly out to their feeding grounds in the mornings when I hear them coming over. Sometimes they are so low, especially in fog, that you can hear the beating of their wings, like the rhythmic swishing of velvet curtains. Other times you can only hear their mournful cries. The other day I was outside when I heard them calling and then I saw them, wave after wave appearing above the horizon, passing rapidly overhead and on out of sight. They fly in a wishbone formation, about thirty in each group I think, though it's hard to count them. Occasionally, much later you'll see a mere one or two flying the same course. Have they overslept? Will they find the others? Probably: a big flock can be heard miles away.

Some of the farmers resent the geese, claiming they spoil crops, but geese often seem to be concentrating on gleaning grain from a stubble field and manuring it heavily as they go. There are fewer stubble fields now that autumn ploughing followed by winter wheat or barley is more common, but this year at least there is still plenty of grass to eat.

We often see the Northern Lights in autumn. The lights are quite diffuse, similar to a city's glow in the sky, but greenish. You need to watch for some time before you see the slow movement: when you do, you understand why they're called The Heavenly Dancers. Late on a very cold moonless night, when the countryside is silent the Northern Lights are very eerie.

The old myths and legends have a powerful reality here: we see the same birds, pick the same berries, follow the same seasons as did people living here thousands of years ago. Stone circles remind us of those folk, and the patterns of speech in Scots—still commonly spoken in the northeast—echo other and older tongues. One of the most poignant reminders of the continuity of human experience is the tales and songs of the travelling people. Mostly itinerant rather than Romany, they have been for centuries both outcast and aloof. They retained the oral tradition of story and ballad even as it died elsewhere. In the 1950s, researchers from the School of Scottish Studies were astounded to find in Buchan living people singing the great ballads of love and death, and telling the ancient stories of the search for truth and wisdom, as part of their everyday entertainment, in much the same manner as people all over the world have done from our beginning. The travelling people have been gradually merged into the larger society as their old way of life—living in tents, moving on—became less and less tenable. Meanwhile the last of the tribe, in their fifties and older, are writing their autobiographies, writing down tales and giving lectures and workshops on the art of storytelling. We went to one such the other night. Stanley Robertson, nephew of the legendary ballad singer Jeannie Robertson, told us about the origin of story and the persecution of the travellers. This was fairly well worn ground and unremarkable; it was when he began to tell us stories that he came into his own. I have heard him in public and private on several occasions, and he never fails to amaze: the mummified remains of tales familiarised by Grimm, assume a unique identity as they come to life in Stanley's words. As with singing, the timing and phrasing are crucial—skills which lift a mere collection of ideas into Art. As we listened, the age-old dilemmas acquired contemporary meaning; we were the eternal audience, listening to the archetypal tales, in this magic land.

CHRISTINE B SIMPSON

Aberdeen on his Tod for Starters Like

He couldn't believe he was doing this: returning to Mrs T's Third Term. After just eight months away. And to Aberdeen, *OF ALL PLACES*, he screamed in sheer, bloody, too-late-now desperation. Not even Glasgow. He was leaving Munich where he had longed, ached, for a real four-year contract. Way before the offer of a job back home materialised, he had caught himself giving it laldy one day as he strode past the Residenz: *Don't stop me now, I'm having such a good time, I'm having a ball.* His attempts to recreate the rock accompaniment in his throat must have perturbed the German bourgeois, but he was oblivious to them. He had sung in vain.

Before he departed for good in September, he showed his German friends his Colin Baxter postcards of Aberdeen. One last time. He wanted them to visit him. He'd bought the cards on the eve of his interview in July. As soon as he arrived in Dyce, in fact. 'Town House Clock Tower at Dusk', 'Fish Market Quay at Dawn', 'Chapel and Crown Tower, King's College' and 'Coat of Arms, King College' all made the desired impression. A quid well invested. He raved about the cobbled Auld Toon. He withheld his own first set of colour prints of the city, but. They were too true-to-life. And anyway, he might as well have used black and white. Grey sky, grey granite. No matter how much he talked to himself, he couldn't see that it was silver. Let's face it: Grampian Transport supplied the only colour—lemon and bright green. On one photo, A BETTER JOB COULD BE RIGHT UP YOUR STREET was splattered along the side of a passing bus. He didn't think it was an omen. He hoped not.

He made a point of telling the Germans about the Aberdonian who moved Cultural History. Even if it was only the girl in the university bookshop. The same one didn't mind English getting narrower and narrower either. It meant she had less to dust. He kept quiet, but, about dragging himself up and down Union Street, looking in vain for something to do other than *Rambo III*. He did mention the bistro *Ici*, and how its seven-feet-tall black bouncer, in black tails and dickie bow, had been joined for a few minutes by his wee black pal, a five-footer in black denim gear and a white T-shirt. But he didn't let on to the Germans that he'd ended up back in his hotel room, playing anagrams with 'Aberdeen'. And supplying cryptic clues for the phrases he came up with. The first one was obvious: 'Lager lout from the North-East?' His favourite was: 'Marie Antoinette's maiden name?' (née Bread).

Aberdeen would be wet and wintry, gey grey, he imagined. So his last weeks in Munich were spent soaking up superb sunshine. Emergency rations for the gloom ahead. He expected fewer hours of daylight up there. Scandinavian conditions. Ah well, he could always glean material for an Ingmar Bergman-type film.

In late September he hit Aberdeen for three days. To hunt for a single room. A low-cost base, as from a week later, from which to look for his first-ever mortgaged flat. As the train returned him to the scene of his greatest triumph, he felt a curious reluctance to celebrate. Outside the station, from the cobbled taxi rank, his eye caught a not-yet-Baxterised cross-section of slated roofs and chimney pots and stacks. Up behind them somewhere was Union Street. It suddenly hit him that this place was to be home-sweet-home, "Just like that!", for the next three years. Hit him hard. (He would be living alone.)—There was nothing for it. He got walking. Chanted "Guild, Market, Union, Broad" as he looked out the advertised route from the station to Tourist Info.

When he got there, he immediately appointed Aberdeen "City of Culture". For the Rest of '88 anyway. Just booking B&B entitled him to free membership of a Leisure Centre for the duration of his visit. Stuff room-hunting. He would try out their sauna that very evening.

He'd discovered and cultivated the habit in Munich. Sauna, steam room, 57 varieties of showers and hoses, rest room, sauna garden in which to saunter. Germans knew how to be good to themselves. The freezing cold plunge, also very Germanic if clichés were to be believed. At the start he counted to ten or, if he'd been taking the brave pills, twenty. Soon it was to 125. One German with a sense of humour had even pleaded, "Goney get oot afore ye warm the water up?"

That had been at a District Council complex on the shores of the lake at Starnberg. While resident in Munich, he wandered along once a week. The massive mountain range at the other end was clearly visible only three times in all those months. The *Föhn* wind drove some people to suicide, but it also brought you nose-to-nose wi they mountains. Forget the zoom lens on days like that. The other lasting image: swans with the neck to go out onto the promenade and stoney beach towering over, and penning in, fragile miniature grannies with gateau-crumbs. Very up-market, Munich, you know. Another image, now he thought of it: the triangle in front of the *Feldherrnhalle*, thronging with body beautifuls and designer labels, yuppified *Übermenschen*, never a blemish, in late after-noon sunshine. That Hitler's *putsch* was crushed there in 1923 remains unmentioned on the plaque. Be thankful for small anti-Fascist guide-books.

In Aberdeen, the sauna lurked behind the bus station. Streets chock-a-block with traffic and fumes. The one-arm-bandits visible through the dark stained-glass doors nearly sent him home again. But in he went and up to the fourth floor. The first shock was Bowie and Jagger belting it out in the torture chamber officially designated 'gym'. Imagine getting your body stretched to that! Then came the telly in the Wet Area, which presumably also functioned as Rest Room. Deafening inside the actual sauna and steam room too. What would Germans make of this? A Rangers-Hearts cup-tie was to be broadcast live. He watched the opening minutes from the jacuzzi. Suddenly the telly was excused.

As he relaxed into an increasingly horizontal state, he was pleasantly bubbled and surged at from more and more directions. Feelings of bliss were spoiled only by Rangers taking an eleventh-minute lead. He was treated to the sight of mainly towel-less bodies racing out the sauna to catch and celebrate the replay. They looked like regular attenders. One guy, skud-naked, went skidding and just about castrated his mate as he tried to grab hold of something. So much for 'taught to be cautious'. The attempted Masonic handshake didn't quite come off. The up-ended punter ended up flat on his face, well inside the Wet Area. Some wit shouted "Penalty!" The referee gave it. He didn't even consult his linesman. Exuberant, the fallen fan saluted the fellow supporters he saw rejoicing in slow motion in the puddles.

The excellent facilities easily out-stripped the expectations created by Munich. He couldn't help thinking back, but, to the German way of things. Here, some of these super-fit Schwarzeneggers smoked cigars between circuits. One punter even had a dogfood-burger plus chips served at his reclining chair. Another guy, grilling himself on a sun-bed, wore only *Blues Brothers* specs and his personal Hi-Fi. What a picture! *Adonis with accessories*. They could use the photie in adverts for Breville Sandwich Toasters.

But chrissake, lads, what about culture, the philosophy, the meditation, the spiritual side? "The SILENCE??", he roared and was asked to leave. Aye, okay, but eh, could ah have a few minutes to get on me first?

Next day the room search started in earnest. The B&B woman offered him his poky hole [£12 a night] for £50 a week, but with just a cereal breakfast. An hour later, in the university Accommodation Register, he found the very same room-in-inverted-commas offered, same terms, for £30. This discrepancy set the tone. Clearly, any private accommodation was B&B for tourists in the vacation, and landlords wanted to squeeze the same cash out of impoverished students, even if it meant three to a room. He phoned to inquire about single rooms at up to £30. Again and again, reluctant voices, feart to give him a knockback in case they lost the business, but too greedy to strike a bargain at the advertised price, conceded that actually they were hoping that come the beginning of term, two students would go halfers on the same room for £40. So much for wanting to resist prejudices about mean Aberdonians. They were at it. Flymen, so they were.

Eventually he was allowed to view one. He'd come immediately. The woman gave him instructions from Union Street. Fifteen minutes, she said. He'd been walking for 1½ hours ("I've started so I'll finish") and reached the Cults Hotel when he established that at best he'd covered half the route. She must have meant by private jet.

Next morning he walked batches of west-end streets, each with numerous possibilities, all extracted from the register the night before. That's academic training for you. He got nothing but soaked and abuse. He thought of pitching a tent in the Beechgrove Garden. One woman, 50-plus, took a shine to him, but had given away her last room by phone the previous day. She couldn't go back on her word. She had reservations, but. The young man from Bel-fast, of all places. "And he could be black for all I know . . .", she said, expecting him to nod in enthusiastic agreement. Twenty minutes later, on another street, he caught himself deliberately going to the house with the Chinese surname last, though it meant doubling back. An attractive redhaired freckled mother opened the door, surrounded by a handful of off-colour bairns with Chinese slants.

He changed tactics (cue: *flexibility*) and entered a telephone box armed with several 20 unit phonecards. He went through the remaining addresses in the bulky register alphabetically. His soaking trousers had dried out by the time he reached W. He was almost replacing the receiver in a by now automatic motion when it clicked that this woman had said yes. By the time he got there, the single room had become a window-less, sink-less, cooker-less kitchen with a microwave and a planned fridge. He would have to share this, the bathroom, and the spacious, well-furnished living-cum-bedroom with the first willing punter to come along. A converted attic. 35 a week. Each. Actually, he wanted a room of his own, but the train back to Glasgow left in a few hours. And he reckoned he'd earned another sauna.

On his fifth day proper in Aberdeen he got to rent a two-bedroom flat, on one of the quaint streets of the dreams he didn't dare to have when he first set eyes on them back in July. The livingroom window looked out on to the Crown atop the Tower of King's College. The MacRobert Memorial and its Astrolabe were beneath him. From his kitchen window he could read the time from the Old Town House clock beyond a chimney stack smothered in blazing ivy. Clear blue skies delivered daily. Warm autumn colours, too, which not even memories of his granny's stair carpet could spoil. The trees dropped their leaves to reveal the towers of St Machar's Cathedral. Solid grey stone attached to a comparatively flimsy wooden clock-face (no protective glass). Munich was now forgotten.

At weekends, he let handsomely produced Tourist Info leaflets determine his routes around the city. The Old Aberdeen Walk introduced him to the Snow Kirkyard (1497), well hidden in the grounds of the Halls, as likely as not never spotted by generations of residential students. Twenty or so graves, including that of a Major's wife, 29 when she died, buried together with the four youngsters aged 5, 2, 40 and 7 months repectively, that she lost in her last seven years.

The gravestone carried the synopsis of a bestseller for the writing. The couple had been so prolific, it might even be a bodice-ripper. Alternatively, he could imagine millions of greatbritish housewives and workless sobbing into their sugared cornflakes as Mister Bates read out the Major's tale-of-woe on Radio 1. Interrupting it to play *Two Little Boys* by Rolf Harris. That would cheer the Major up. No end.

At King's College, an antiquated sign recorded fines in pre-decimal shillings and pence for smoking, defacing the property, walking on the grass, and riding bicycles in the quadrangle. The Tillydrone Road, beneath trees whose roots didn't take no for an answer when up against a brick wall, led him to the Wallace Tower, named after the Guardian of Scotland, but moved from its original city centre site to make way for

Marks and Sparks. Through Seaton Park he reached the salmon fishers' cottages flanking the Brig o' Balgownie. *To live in hearts we leave behind is not to die.* The beach esplanade lay beyond a noisy road. The setting sun yellowed the crests of the waves. Gulls with ferocious wingspangs screech voraciously.

The model fishing village of Footdee ('Fittie') reminded him of Övelgönne in Hamburg. Pocra Quay, the Round House, the harbour. A trio of lighthouses. Turds trundled out from beneath the North Pie ·. Jobbies bobbing towards Torry. It was okay, but. He didn't think th ·y would have the strength to climb out on the other side of the narrow waterway. And even if they did, cars would get the wee shites as they crossed the Greyhope Road. What's more, small hard white spherical bombs would blast them off the Balnagask Golf Course if they tried to take Torry from the hills.

He walked back a few paces. Spotted the *Silver Darling* fish restaurant, with its main courses starting at ten quid a time, described in mouth-watering French but. Even he felt tempted, though put off fish for life by about five years of pre-Vatican II Fridays.

Via Waterloo Quay, Regent Quay, and Shiprow, and turned on by the whole damn thing, he made his way back to Old Aberdeen. Four hours he'd been out. And he'd touched upon at least three of the official walks. His camera had been doing overtime. Bastardised Baxters.

Okay, he gave in, he liked the place. Loved it, even. On top of all this, a cooperative Superstore supplied good food he'd feared he'd left behind in Munich. Continental cheeses. No call yet for listeria hysteria. Haricot beans, chick peas. 'Fresh Soured Cream' for German soups, great, wee man. Horseradish. Greek yoghurt with banana, muesli, and sunflower seeds for breakfast. (His breakfast table still bore the mark of his last long-term girlfriend)—And ya beauty: Italian *Dolci*, chocolate flavoured cookies, almost sponge-like texture, with chocolate chips. The girl at the cash-out said, "It's nice to see someone with different taste". She charged him the full whack nonetheless.

He did without a telly. Even the classical tones broadcast by Radio 3 could seem like noise pollution, but, and bug him something awful. He listened to Handel's *Water Music* in the bath. A Desmond Wilcox TV programme he happened to catch the start of wasted Pachelbel's *Canon* on him. Nothing could beat Samuel Barber's *Adagio for Strings*, its gentle elegiac theme winding, but with an undeniable forward momentum, from one voice to another; gaining in body, involving more and more of the orchestra in the process; a touch of the old *post coitum omne animal triste*; and yet, when the piece peaked, with rearing violins, not just on their overstretched hind legs but almost toppling from a precarious pirouette, it was obvious that there had been no previous climax, and that now there should, and would, be no climax; screech on the brakes; straining, restrained, restraint.

He read. He scribbled. He had to find some way of easing the pressure of his planned mortgage. Staying in to read and write meant he didn't spend money. Literature kept him off the streets. Was that a politically defensible attitude?

Apropos of politics. Even within his first weeks in Aberdeen, all kinds of crazy things happened. (1) Thatcher turned Green. God knows what colour Franz Josef Strauss turned when (2) he put on his wooden pyjamas; God knows if God cared. (3) Very English Sunday newspapers started introducing Scottish supplements. (4) The government imposed a ban on broadcasting interviews with terrorists. (5) The same government discussed whether defendants in court should still have the right to remain silent. (6) Trade Union membership for GCHQ workers in Cheltenham was scrapped. (7) The SNP won Govan. (8) The Speaker of the West German Parliament resigned after a controversial speech on the 50th anniversary of *Kristallnacht*. And (9) the Russians were coming—round. It was all a bit much at once. Hard to keep track. His copious, unfiled newspaper cuttings helped a little. Stopping to work it all out wasn't on, but. He had to have a mortgaged roof over his head by December 31. It went with the salary, the right to pay income tax for the first time at the age of 27-and seven-twelfths, and the Protected Short Tenancy of his rented flat.

"Do you know anything about buying a house?" one solicitor asked, hardly waiting for an answer before jerking into action. Just like the Laughing Policeman in the glass booth at fairgrounds. There followed a pre-recorded message, or what sounded like one. Their eyes hardly met. At the end of the glib spiel, there being no questions, there having been no communication, the solicitor ceased to solicit, went limp, drooped, dummy-like. A building society rep was not so pre-prepared. When explaining the intricacies of the financial arrangements, he paused after every second phrase, then said "Aye—" before continuing. Had he convinced himself that he'd got it right so far? And that the next bit would be accurate too? That was nice to know.

It was strange to hear big money being discussed professionally but with large doses of dialect. Were these guys' qualifications recognised nationally? Or did they deliver milk, sell fresh eggs, and knit traditional patterns in the afternoons and evenings? Almost immediately the building society's local hero had said, "You'll be from the South?" Personally, he had never thought of the West of Scotland as 'the South'. 'Down South' was Maggie's territory. Yet soon he himself would be using the phrase to refer to home in Glasgow. It was weird not understanding folk from your own country. Weirder still when the speaker was sharing the same sauna, steam room, or jacuzzi. He'd felt less out of place in Bavaria. Even when they wore funny hats and leather shorts. He took refuge in Glaswegianisms.

There was the minor matter of finding a suitable property. He walked it. Armed with a Street Atlas and Property Centre print-outs he scouted Aberdeen on foot. It was becoming his. He soon knew it more intimately than any other city. He opted for a turn-of-the-century brothel, known locally as the 'Dolls' House' (apologies to Ibsen). The address contained his lucky number. Twice. Plus, it was the best two-bedroom flat going. First recorded 175 years earlier, the present, now converted, four-storey building was approximately 100 years old. Unattached, as befits a brothel, it stood high above the street. From the nearby Don, smugglers used to row through underground passages into the cellar, he heard. A tall house with many a tale. His German friends would love it. The ghosts would be a barrel of laughs. Maybe they could go into business together and sell Haunted Orgies to tourists. Boo-jobs in a quondam brothel had to be worth something. The setting was bang-on. The cobbles lent the area an aura of the ancient and traditional. Internally, the house possessed yet more original features: a stone-gravel hallway, or so the clatty carpet made it seem; a lounge with an unusual beamed ceiling, and an open pine stairway to the first floor; views of Aberdeen Bay from both bedroom windows; wallpaper with a sense of humour—he planned to do a lot of stripping in his former brothel! On the day he moved in, Mrs Edwina Currie MP resigned. Ach well, she'll have had her Christmas bonus.

DONAL McLAUGHLIN

New Year Speyside

On Hogmanay, first footers came from the distillery cottages. Our boys slept through it all, even when the mashman was found playing with the train set laid out on their bedroom floor. The brewer had already tried to exit through the kitchen cupboard.

URSULA STOALING

Spirit of Nova Scotia
Folk Art at Aberdeen Art Gallery

Here everyman's a woodturner
Whittling away testimonies of his life
from logs which cling to their past
of root and branch

Scarlet cows dance on wood-knotted hooves
To tunes which set small couples in
static squares
Chaperoned by their steel-pinned arms,
Watched by a leering mountie whom
frost or a loveless heart has
split down the trunk

In this New Land
we see ourselves through the looking-glass
where everything is childs-eye bright

House-high horses prance in Inverness
And cats come fiddling through
Antigonish town
Where a pink-winged pig flies brazenly by
a somnolent owl

Have you ever seen a wowl?

Asks the storytelling quilt
whose mice and mottoes creep
into the child's nighttime world
As the cockerel spins to sleep on
his holy perch

The rest dance on
to the devil's own tune
Following the steps of the girl and dog
who go waltzing past
Desire dancing stiff between them

And the woman who haunts the dreams
of Collins Eisenhower
gives a knowing glance
Baring her real teeth in an ingratiating smile
While her clamped arms hold a strip
of painted modesty across her breasts

This is a land of fishing-tale truths
whose values grow with the dark winter nights
and who knows if reality had the last laugh
with the carver of dreams

Or the owner of the teeth.

ALISON DUNCAN

Chicago Aberdeen Arbroath

It was odd that Aberdeen should enter
His thoughts then, incongruous as the precentor
Watching 'Top of the Pops', as the sirens
Wailed down Erie and environs,
Oblivious to Britain's number one
And the Free Kirk; and to the sun
Mooching his way westward over Scotland,
Observing a hundred morning coffees (What land
Does not claim her sun as her own?) But it did,
Odd though it was. Below him, the grid
Stretched out like an infinite cushion south,
Till the lights merged into a fuzzy mouth
Whispering neon sweet nothings through the clinging,
Sour, breathless, hot, singing
Broth. He chuckled over the ignorant city,
Thinking of an old story which Aunt Kitty
Knew, about the man who asked if Granny
Was in; "I'm sorry," he was told. "Ye cannae
See her—she's at Arbroath." "That's fine,"
He said, "I'll wait till she's feenished." The line
Giggled down Madison, and in downtown Big Macs,
Cackled in China town and sleepless fax

Machines, laughing with intimate friends
In New York Paris London, ends
Of the Earth, Moscow, Tokyo, Aberdeen:
The newest stop on the global scene
For oil and herring. The thought was so daft
That the couple below looked up as he laughed
Till he cried and cried, but with more sorrow
Than mirth in the tears tumbling into to-morrow
Where was home in this city? laid bare
Like a centrefold before him, yet greyer
And more inscrutable than a fishwife
Looking East; a crawling still life
With 'WET PAINT' scrawled on the sidewalk.
He dare not touch . . .
                              He woke with a shock.
Light blared insolently past his head
Bleary with dried tears. Quietly he shed
His clothes, unwilling to wake any more,
Wrapped a towel round, and closed the door
Softly behind, moving toward the shower room.
As the water spattered down warm, he wondered whom
He'd meet to-day: preachers speaking
Of your soul and alcohol; buskers seeking
Pennies from businesspeople deep
In conference and a tuna sub, and a heap
Of kids rolling past crosslegged blind, their upturned
Hats full of Coca-Cola cans spurned
By the good and evil alike. There was no home
In this city, but the people and the streets to roam,
And Aberdeen entered his thoughts again
As he scuffed his way East at ten after ten.

DONALD MacEWAN

Indecision

It's lang syne noo since first I cam' tae bide near Aiberdeen
The widder wis atrocious—goodbye tae high-heeled sheen.
I had mixed feelin's a can tell, aboot this countryside
I wisnae a'fa trickit wi't, an' thocht—I winna bide.

Wi' goods an' chattels we arrived tae find an open hoose
Oor welcomin' committee wis a bricht ee'd little moose.
A coal fire flickered in the grate an' beckoned us inside
But a' the time a'm thinkin'—na na, I winna bide.

I hidna been here but a wik fan, man, the widder changed
I struggled oot ma bed a' day an' thocht a wis deranged.
The ice wis half inch thick an' mair, an' that wis jist inside
I dived back in ma bed an' cried—nae fears, I winna bide.

The sna' cam neist, it wisna real, I'd niver seen the like
I lookit oot the windae an' couldna see the dyke.
Three wiks gied by an' ilka day a hid tae keep inside
An' mair determined than before, says I—I winna bide.

A licence was a must noo, an' I hid tae buy a car
It wis a real essential cause the shop an' skweel's oor far.
There wis nae names tae twisty roads tae help gie ye a guide
T'wis mair than eence that I got tint—na na, I winna bide.

In summer time the wall gied dry, it happened wi'oot fail
I hid tae wa'k for half a mile wi' watter in a pail.
At nicht I'd crawl intae ma' bed tae find a'd raxed ma side
This country life is afae hard—na na, I winna bide.

Fan animals come on the go ye say goodbye tae leisure
But they are weel wirth a' the chav, they gie ye as much pleasure.
There's calves an' sheep an' dogs an' cats, an' horses here tae ride
But if a canna manage them—I dinna hae tae bide.

I've dune an afa lot o' things a niver thocht a could
Fae ploughman, vet an' plumber tae, tae sawin' up the wood.
The frozen neeps stuck tae ma hands the tappiner gied aglie
An' muckin' oot wis hivvy wirk—na na, I winna bide.

The years rolled on, the wains grew up, things dinna bide the same
The crofts an' beasts are o' the past, an' noo I'm on ma ain.
It's twinty 'ear an' mair noo since I first saw Ythanside
Some day a micht get used tae it, fa kens?—I'll maybe bide.

EVELYN GORDON

Deeside—Early Morning

We cruise along a road flanked first by houses and shops then suddenly by flowers, fields and trees. Signposts jabbed into the verge remind us we are in Scotland proclaiming, 'Drum Castle', 'Farm Shop', 'Free Range Eggs', 'Tatties', 'Heather Centre', 'Crathes Castle' and the suchlike. Our heads twist this way and that, earnestly hoping to steal a glimpse of one of these monuments, but tantalisingly the signs always point down narrow tracks leading away between the bleak clumpy grassed fields into the distance where nothing is visible. The sun lurking behind the hills, suddenly creeps out at us, dabbling these translucent grey skies with shocking-pink brush strokes, a burst of orange exploding, bringing the dark blue landscape to a life of greens and yellows. The colours reflect from the faces of my family gazing in wonderment at the view, their grey pallor gives way to a glow, as they sit three-in-a-row, pink tinged cheeks and eyes sparkling. I have the feeling of receiving some absurd good news. I want to sing, I want to hug my family close.

The taxi stops. We have arrived.

I look down across the sleeping valley, the mist burning away in the golden light. The asymetrical patchwork quilt of red, gold, dark-green, yellow trees . . .

I think back to my first brief visit to Aberdeen two months earlier.

A long bumpy seat-belted propeller-driven flight from Humberside in the rain. Disgorged, hungover and tired. The taxi-driver told me, "Nice day". I looked out between the rain drops chasing down the windows forming relief maps of rivers and islands, at the incessant drizzle. I looked back at the weather-beaten and rugged face for the sign of a smile which would betray a joke. Stone-faced. I began to wonder whether he was serious. There is a terrifying feeling of helplessness, the first time in a new city, as you give yourself over to the system. This taxi could be going anywhere. I knew no landmarks, all I could see were the drab grey granite buildings. The churches, reaching out in vain over the flat skyline, poking spires into the gloom. Here and there, huge new buildings, shouting 'Oil, Oil, Oil!' but somehow complimentary to this peculiar, beached city. I had imagined it bigger, industrialised, belching sulphurous fumes across a brown-rinsed sky. This contradiction of offices, docks, rivers, gardens and beaches was beyond the stretch of my imagination. We turned a corner and cruised along Union Street in five minutes, from end to end. Oh, just try that in London, the length of Oxford Street in five minutes! Impossible, where were the legions of red buses and black cabs to impede our progress? Where were the glowering looks and silent abuse mouthed through tinted windows? The violent matador's dance of accelerator and brake? This was a new world. I had thought Lincolnshire an oasis of manners in a desert of spite, but it had no genteel city like this.

This then, was Aberdeen to me. A gritty, grey, granite metropolis. Travelling out to Peterculter, the impression is of a built-up mass of humanity, stretching for miles in every direction. I could not see then that this was just an arm outstretched toward the Grampians.

I was duped. Later, flying over Aberdeen at night I saw the true boundaries of the city lit in a network of earthbound stars, the long arm pointing invitingly to those dark humps glooming in the distance.

Never in our wildest dreams . . . Now, as the dawn chorus began to reach its crescendo and the postman passing gave us a cheery but inquiring wave, we turned as if in slow motion and crossed the threshold. Glancing over our shoulders, we checked to make sure that the view was still there, that this was not a dream, that we were in the here and now.

The taxi driver was right. We had arrived.

MALCOLM FAWCETT

Migrant

The seagulls are soaring outside my window again, like white floating papers caught in a whirlwind. They are my reminder that I am near the sea. I forget that when I look out of my window at the endless apartment blocks—granite boxes holding life. A sturdy substance to surround such treasure. In Chicago the buildings are made of soot, splintered wood and broken glass. Life leaks out on to straight streets and gutters. No-one seems to care in that city, the windy city, the city I came from.

A warm wind whistles outside my window. Spring comes early here. Crocus and daffodils in March—a pleasant surprise for me. I am used to grey days until May. I long to get out and walk in the forest. The greenness there glows with unbelievable energy. The mosses and lichens explode at each angle of branch. Mysterious bird calls of courting drift down from above. It's not far from here. To have country so close. And the mountains are like a dream, something I never before experienced. Miles and miles of moors and mountains and streams. Life at home in the valleys. No more walls pushing, people pushing—freedom at last. I can run and run and run. No sprawling city. No buildings that rise up to the sky. The land of the free? Home of Mickey Mouse? Not for me. No, not for me!

People here glow with life—not like the barely breathing figures in the city I knew, avoiding the sun and the air and running into their skyscraper holding their heads. No weathering there. No glow. No life. Only the skyscrapers looking down on the heap of humanity.

Chicago is just a book on a coffee-table now. Chaos clamped into flat glossy pages—a manageable form. So I can relax here with tea and think of tomorrow and hope for a card in the post. I hear a seagull and think of the granite city edged with sea. A stable place for now. I hope the buildings stay sturdy and low and old. They must keep the feeling of their people and past. A seagull cries again. I look out and see a new tall highrise reaching further towards the sky, away from the people, away from the land. America slowly creeping in!

AMY STERLY

Spikkin' Toons

Ken ess?

I think thon blokes 'at bilt the medieval pier,
And them that beereet a' their gear
In front o' Marks & Sparks,
Spoke jist like you and me.

(a bittie mair aul-fashent mebbe)

But learned men in ivory towers shake heads dismissively.
'Town's speech? Debased, corrupt, bastardised.'

(Hey watch it min)

'Only the honest men of the soil speaks the authentic language of the North-East.'

Well ah'm nae shod in sharny beets,
Nor o'er the heid wi' dung.
But is that ony reason why
My song should nae be sung?

Fit kin' o' language wis there then,
Fan Machar's too'ers were biggit.
Fit kin o spik amongst the men,
Fan clipper ships were riggit?

Fa brocht their bairns up, sent them oot
Fan they were jist bit loons,
Tae mak their mark o'er a' the world,
Still maistly Spikkin 'Toons'.

So—nae authentic?—gie't a miss,
Awa' an' bile yer heid.
We'll be Spikkin' jist like iss,
Lang efter yoo're a' deid.

Onywye—

An Honest Fairmer

Fit's 'at?

SHEILA ELDER

Glenlivet Memories

At that time, life in Glenlivet revolved mainly around whisky-making (and drinking!) farming and forestry. On my arrival, I quickly found aspects of the glen lifestyle which I thought should be improved, but the locals were equally determined to convince me that their way was right and best. In my job as Customs and Excise Officer I was often up against the seemingly God-given right of some of the distillery employees and others to acquire a sippie of the hard stuff; an uneasy truce existed most of the time, as their idea of moderation and mine differed substantially.

The methods used to extract the whisky, mature and immature, were many and varied. In one case, Jockie, one of the stillmen, bored through the top of a spirit-carrying pipe and inserted a rivet to plug the hole when it was not in use for illicit purposes. This rivet was then whitewashed to simulate pigeon-droppings, the whole exercise being calculated to deceive the gauger. Unfortunately, when the spirit vapour started along the pipe and escaped past the rivet, a fairly loud, strange, unfamiliar whistling noise was heard. It was well-known that Jockie, the afore-mentioned stillman was no whistler—he was practically toothless!—and his resignation was tendered and accepted on the spot.

Another case of over-indulgence came to light when a warehouseman, seen emerging unsteadily from the warehouse proclaiming to all and sundry that he'd only had "a toothfu'", fell flat on his face and was taken at speed to Aberdeen Royal Infirmary for treatment by stomach pump.

The subject of the demon drink always loomed large at Christmas and Hogmanay. One year the local District Nurse volunteered to produce a unique drink for the occasion—skeachan! Unfortunately, she was laid low with a bad bout of 'flu during the manufacturing period and the brew acetified—(went vinegary!). There was no time to make a repeat brew, so around eight pounds of brown sugar were added to mask the original (awful!) taste. As no-one knew what skeachan should taste like, there were few complaints, but no compliments either!

ANDY DUFF

Inverness Quine

Bakery shops were the bane of my life. During my first few weeks here I never once left Mitchell & Muill's with the items I went in to buy. I'd go in for four rolls and come out with four butteries, till one day I plucked up courage to challenge the hefty lady behind the counter.

"Why do you always give me butteries when I want rolls for sandwiches?" I pleaded.

"Rolls is rowies here", came the short, sharp reply. "If ye're wantin' safties, ask for safties or baps, but rolls is rowies".

How I longed to be home again where butteries were butteries, softies were soft biscuits and rolls were thing you used to make sandwiches. From then on I learned to point to what I wanted, but bakery shops still fill me with dread. I doubt if I'll ever master the language of the rowie or the funcy piece.

But from the start I was otherwise made so very welcome; and although, even now, I can't do a word for-word-translation, I've progressed a lot since those early days. At least now I know that the answer to "Foo's yer doos?" is "Aye pickin'" and not "I'm sorry, I don't have any pigeons"!

MARY H M NICOLL

Home Thoughts

Noo I lang to hear a teuchat call or yet a larkey sing,
A groose cry thro' a gloamin' sky her young anes hame to bring
Jist to see again at sunset on the eve o' a simmer's day,
The boaties sailin' roon the coast a heidin' for the bay.

Oh, to tramp again doon thro' the moss when the heather's in full bloom.
Or to see a dyke or hedge ablaze wi' the yallow o' the broom.
To tread some lush green meadow in the springtime o' the year,
Or feel a dewy mornin' when the craps begin to brier
These are jist a few o't things I've missed doon thro' the years,
An' ilka time I think o' them my eyes well up with tears.
So I'll pack my kist, an' book my flight an' fly across the main,
Back to dear aul' Buchan an' my ain folk aince again.

                                        MARGARET A LORIMER

Glossary

aglie   off the straight, squint
backie   back-green or back-court of tenements
beereet   buried
biggit   built
binkie   hob
blaw   exaggerate own importance, behave arrogantly
bleed   blood
blethered   talked idly
blin' smorr   whiteout
bowies   bowls
brander   a gridiron for cooking or baking
bree   liquid in which something has been steeped or boiled
breeks   trousers
brier   first shoots of grain etc.
caad   pushed, forced through, kept moving
calkin'   making pay
causie steens   cobblestones
chaain'   chewing
chav/tchav   struggle
chessil   cheese mould
chiel   lad
clipin'   telling who is to blame for something
clockin'/clokkin'   broody
couthie   comfortable, pleasant
craps   crops
dichtin'   wiping
dottled   witless
druchted   drunken
eese   use
fan   when
fashious   angry, bad-tempered
fecht   fight
fee'd   having been hired for work as a servant, usually on a farm
feel   fool
fegs (na fegs)   no indeed
fest   fast
fin/fan   when
fit wye   why
fitin's   whitings (fish)

fleer floor
fleg fright
freen friend
furled whirled
fuskie whisky
fyowe few
fyte white
gangly long-legged and thin
gansie thick woollen jumper worn by fishermen
gie very
gird hoop (plaything)
girny complaining
girse gorse
grat cried
grubber harrow
gweed good
hairst harvest
haivered hovered
hames pieces of wood on the collar of a draught horse
happit wrapped up
hard fish dried or salted fish
hottered bubbled, boiled steadily
humph to carry a heavy or awkward load with difficulty or effort
ilk each
kist wooden storage chest
lickin' hiding
lousin' time/lowsin' time time to stop work
lum chimney
kye cattle
mappie's mou's antirrhinum, calceolaria etc. (flower-heads in the shape of a
   rabbit's mouth)
maun must
moggins indoor footwear
muckle large
murlin round narrow-mouthed basket used by fishermen/women
neep turnip
neives fists
neuk corner
nott need
palin' fence
partans crabs
peenies aprons
piece sandwich
placie euphemism for 'lavatory'
pow head
quiles coals
quine girl
raxed strained
redded/reddin' clear, disentangle, unravel